CONTENTS

UNLEASHED FROM ALCOHOL: UNDERSTAND THE REAL REASON YOU DRINK AND HOW TO HEAL YOURSELF

By Craig Beck

Ready to quit drinking AND transform your life in one amazing weekend? See Craig Beck live at Quit Drinking Bootcamp: www.StopDrinkingExpert.com

The information contained in this book is for general information purposes only. The information is provided by Craig Beck Media and while we endeavor to present information that is up to date and correct, we make no representations or warranties of any kind, express or implied, about the completeness, accuracy, reliability, suitability or availability with respect to the website or the information, products, services, or related graphics contained on the website for

INTRODUCTION

Alcohol is the strangest drug on planet earth! It's the only substance that when you develop a problem with it, they blame you and not the drug. Smokers are not branded life long 'smokeaholics'. Do you insist that any of your friends who have successfully quit smoking may only ever refer to themselves as 'recovering smokeaholics'?

No, of course not, because society understands that nicotine is highly addictive and big tobacco companies are devious and narcissistic in their marketing. When it comes to alcohol, the rules somehow change – your inability to not get addicted to a highly addictive substance apparently means that you are broken.

For over a decade Craig Beck has been deconstructing the illusion of problem drinking and in doing so has helped hundreds of thousands of people around the world to get the happy sober version of themselves back.

The secret to his success is understanding that often alcohol use is not the problem but rather just a symptom of a bigger problem. Many drinkers are using alcohol as a Band-Aid for more profound issues. Some are using it as a sedative to keep past trauma buried. To others, it helps push away the pain of loneliness, anxiety or an unhappy relationship. Some are even using it to cope with physical pain.

The reason other solutions to problem drinking fail so often is they attempt to take away the symptom without addressing the underlying problem. If you are miserable in an unhappy relationship and somebody takes away the thing that was helping you cope, it should be easy to see that your new-found sobriety is a house built without foundations and will quickly crumble and fall.

In this special edition of Unleashed, Craig takes you through the same process he takes his Quit Drinking Bootcamp attendees through. You will discover:

1. The reasons why you drink and how to find a more effective solution.
2. How to love yourself more and unlock your full potential.
3. What your true purpose and calling in life is
4. How to remove lifelong limiting beliefs and live life like you mean it.
5. Ways to replace alcohol with more positive and enjoyable activities.

SECTION ONE –
UNLEASHED FROM
ALCOHOL

WHAT'S YOUR PROBLEM?

There is a vast difference between being dry and being sober. If you have (or perhaps still are) struggling with problem drinking, then you may assume that if you remove the attractively packaged poison from your life then everything will get better. You are not alone in that hope. Many a worried family member has got prematurely excited just because their loved one agreed to go into rehab. They assumed that once the drug was removed, then the person they care about would return happy and carefree. Sometimes this happens, but not always.

Alcoholics Anonymous remains our go-to solution for alcohol addiction. For some, it is a lifesaver, but for many even if they do manage to defy the odds and stay away from the booze, they find sobriety to be a miserable existence. Many approaches to problem drinking are effective in the short-term, but they miss the point somewhat. Inappropriate alcohol use is not the problem that needs to be fixed but it is the symptom of a broader issue. So many people are just unhappy and are using alcohol to escape reality. The reason for that unhappiness is as varied and unique as each human being on the planet. Some people are still haunted by trauma from their childhood, bad stuff that got repressed in the subconscious mind. Others are bored and lonely; I speak to a lot of middle-aged drinkers suffering from empty nest syndrome. Their whole life was about raising and caring for children, then one day the kids became adults and left a huge vacuum behind.

Many people have this constant ache within themselves that they are here to do something meaningful, something significant but can't for the life of them work out what it is. This sort of existential vacuum is painful and uncomfortable – alcohol dulls the noise somewhat. The only problem is using alcohol to deal with this issue is a bit like using a loan shark to deal with your debt problem. Initially, it appears to help but long term you will find yourself in a much deeper hole. Eventually, you will end up at my website complaining of poor health, terrible relationships and a whole host of other problems. You will want me to show you how to stop drinking, and I will. However, if you fail to fix the pain underneath your drinking, you are going to fit into a category of people that we call 'Dry Drunks.' It means you are free of alcohol, but you are still miserable. Naturally, this is not an outcome you want to be aiming for.

My Unleashed range of books and courses came about as a result of meeting far too many people who are constantly beating themselves up and failing to see the magic they have inside themselves. I wanted to help people to unlock their full potential but more importantly, start to love themselves more. When I wrote Unleashed, I intended it to be an entirely separate and stand-alone product to my quit drinking courses and live seminars. However, the more I travel around the world meeting and helping problem drinkers the more I realized that alcoholism is for the most part just the symptom of a much bigger problem. Life is often a struggle, and unfortunately, we are programmed to take the path of least resistance. The irony is that almost everything in life worth having is held just outside our comfort zone, a long way from the easy road we prefer to walk.

In this specially edited and updated version of Unleashed, I am going to show you how to heal yourself from the inside out. In the past, you have thrown buckets of alcohol over the issues that really need to be dealt with rather than putting them under the spotlight. This book (and indeed day two of Quit Drinking Bootcamp) is all about doing just that! If that sounds scary, don't worry because only good things are coming. I know this from my own experience with this nasty little drug. When I finally stopped drinking the attractively packaged poison and got the mental clarity to put my miserable life under the microscope, it became crystal clear what I needed to do to fix it. I learned to accept who I am and all my baggage, I invested in myself and discovered the real value that lies within me. More than anything I learned to love myself just as I am, allowing the pain and self-doubt to fade away. I no longer needed a sedative to avoid my negative and limiting beliefs because I had finally made peace with them. This beautiful state of mind is the same gift I am offering to you today.

I Am Here To Fit You With Some New Glasses

When people ask me what I do for a living, I used to tell them I was a self-help author or a coach. Boring answer, right? These days I tell these nosy folk that I am a unusual type of optician and I fit people with special magic glasses. If you wear spectacles, you will understand the pure joy of 'new glasses day.' The day you go to collect your new prescription from the store, and the optician fits them carefully to match the features of your face. When all the tinkering is done you step out of the optical store into the sunshine and take a few moments to stare in wonder at the sight before you. You are shocked by how bright, crisp and sharp everything looks. It's amazing; it's like you suddenly got an upgrade to high definition eyes.

Of course, nothing has really changed out there on the sidewalk. That super HD world always existed, it's just before walking into the store you had forgotten what it looked like. Now with your new glasses on, your perception of the world has changed. Yes, this is a metaphor for what happens to Super HD, amazing individuals the world over. We come into the world a blank canvas capable of absolutely anything and everything. However, slowly over time, our perception of life fades, distorts and degrades.

As we go through the stages of development, we are taught many things. Some things positively serve us, but others create limiting beliefs that hold us back. The world slowly starts to lose its hard edges, the colors lose their depth and what was once bright becomes dim.

Some people wish they had more self-confidence, or even worse than that, they witness the positive self-image they want in somebody else and get jealous of them. They act like that other person got a better deal of the deck. Perhaps born with little something that was held back for the chosen few. Let me tell you here and now; babies are not born confident. There has never been a midwife hold up a screaming newborn and say Oh, no this poor child has been born with no confidence.' Equally, babies are not born with more than their fair share of confidence either. If today, as an adult you are lacking confidence, this is only because you are wearing the wrong glasses. Your view of yourself is out of focus in this area, and that's all! The fantastic news is you have stumbled upon a book by one of the best fitters of new specs in the world.

We are all born with infinite potential, on that day when we come screaming into the world, nothing is impossible for us. In that moment and for not long after the boundaries of our future are limitless. I know even now, so early on this journey, some readers will be thinking. But what about people born into poverty or with disabilities? Those thoughts are houses built on sand, they appear to stand up to inspection but what I will demonstrate in this book is that they are limiting beliefs without foundations. If pressed I am sure you can think of someone born with severe disabilities who have gone on to achieve amazing things in their life. It is equally as likely that you will be able to think of many more people who have no physical challenges, who were born into the safety, wealth and abundance of civilized western life that have decided to become an abject failure.

Our limiting beliefs are all lies, every single one of them. I tell people that I can't dance, that is a lie. The truth is I have never really tried, I am afraid I might look silly, and so I have created plausible deniability to ensure that I never risk being in that situation. As a species, we are motivated by only two overriding factors. The desire to move towards pleasure or the need to move away from pain. Two very laudable goals and entirely understandable but it's essential that you know that the two objectives are as opposite as black and white. They may sound similar, and I will admit that escaping a painful situation could easily be misinterpreted as being 'pleasurable.' However, only one of these actions serves us in a positive away.

Moving towards pleasure is an empowering, positive action. Pushing away pain and discomfort is an act that may have a purpose, in some situations it may even save your life but it is a generally disempowering act. In my case, creating the limiting belief that I can't dance as a means to protect myself from the embarrassment of trying does not serve or empower me. In truth, I watch people dancing and feel envious of their ability to be so at ease with themselves, to be so free and happy to do something like that in public. So while my firmly held and argued belief that I am incapable of dancing serves a purpose it most certainly does not serve me.

I am quite an unusual guy, I know this, and I kind of like that about me. I am writing this book in Bangkok, Thailand. I have been on an intensive NLP training program for the last ten days. One of the other participants, an amazing and inspirational woman called Grace, has told me on no less than ten occasions that I am not normal. Thankfully, every time she has also laughed and cheekily added 'in a good way.' One of the reasons for that label is my claim that I remember being born. Okay, so it's not like I can remember what I was thinking during the hours of my birth, but I can remember the trauma it caused me. For about the first seven years of my life, I had a recurring nightmare; it happened at least several times a week. The dream was always the same, the sensation of being squeezed until I could no longer breathe along with a strong, unpleasant metallic taste in my mouth and nose. This recurring nightmare would wake me in a cold sweat so routinely I almost accepted it as just a part of what happens at night. As a dream it made no sense, that is until I worked out what it was.

We worry a whole heap about dying, but I suspect our birth is the more traumatic event in our life. Our subconscious mind is amazing, and one of its many millions of roles is to repress traumatic emotional events that we are not equipped to deal with. Many young victims of sexual abuse can recall no detail of what happened to them because of this unique function of the human brain. I am reasonably sure that being born is one of the most horrific things that we ever experience, and this traumatic event will end up being our first repression. That's why you probably don't remember being born, and you should trust me on this - you are not missing anything good.

However, I am digressing somewhat from the point. When I was born, I can assure you that the midwife did not frown as she presented me to my exhausted mother. She did not have an expression of concern, and a doctor was not called to break the news to my parents that unfortunately I had been born without the ability to dance. Nobody advised my family that it would be pointless even to try because I would never be able to do the Macarena no matter how hard I worked. What this means is at some point I decided that I could not dance, I repeated it so many times that it stopped being a statement and became a limiting belief. As I previously mentioned all of these beliefs are nothing more than lies (the world believe even has the word lie right in the middle as a big fat hairy clue).

There are things that you firmly believe about yourself that are equally as erroneous. When I walk onto the stage at one of my live UNLEASHED events I can never tell what has brought each person to me. Some people want to deal with the low self-confidence, some want to improve the quality of their relationships, many need some encouragement to take a risk and get started with their own business and often people are there because they know, deep down that they are capable of so much more. Whatever brought them to that event and whatever brought you to this book is almost certainly a lie. That's a statement that upsets a lot of people. It's true that many people have had super tough challenges and obstacles in their life. It may seem that someone with a profound physical disability has a compelling justification for not living their dreams. You are welcome to cling onto that if it serves you in any way, but I already know that it doesn't.

My son Jordan was born in Sharoe Green Hospital, Preston England on 14th September 1997. In the bed next to my ex-wife, Denise was a woman called Julia Moore. She gave birth to a baby girl the very same afternoon that my son was born, they called her Bethany. During the labor Julia and Denise had become firm friends. They supported and encouraged each other throughout the contractions and pain of giving birth. When Jordan was born, we were so overcome with our joy and happiness that we failed to notice that Julia had not returned to the ward. After a while, we asked where she was and were told that there had been a problem with the birth and Julia and her baby had been taken to intensive care.

When Bethany was born the doctors noticed a strange lump

pushing outward from her spine. The concern on the faces of the midwives said it all and doctors immediately began to work on little Beth to determine precisely what was going on. Julia had to endure months of weekly hospital visits before she finally got an answer. The senior consultant sat her down one day and explained that the lump was a massive tumor. Unfortunately, cancer had wrapped itself around Bethany's spinal cord, and while they could operate to remove some of it, it would be impossible to remove it all. It was a tidal wave of bad news after bad news that day. Julia was told that Bethany would never be able to walk but worse than that her chances of living more than a few years were practically zero.

When life deals us a bad hand, whether it's something as insignificant as spilling our morning coffee into our lap on the commute into work or what Bethany had to face we tend to feel like life is unfair or that we are cursed with bad luck. The truth, of course, is life is all about the struggle; it's about getting knocked down over and over again. That is inevitable, and if you spend your life trying to avoid it, you will only become more and more depressed at your inability to control the uncontrollable.

It doesn't matter how wealthy, confident or personally centered you get the knockdowns are going to come and sometimes they are going to feel like they could be knock out's. The only choice you will ever get is whether you get back up or stay down on the mat. This is the only accurate measure of success in my opinion. We tend to judge our performance in life by comparing what we accomplish to what we see others achieving. We pre-decide that if we are doing better than our neighbor, then we are a success, less than him means we are a big fat failure. This is a huge source of misery and a dangerous misconception that is propagated and amplified by Hollywood and the media. We are bombarded with the message that anything less than perfect is a failure. You must be a high flyer in your career while maintaining a slim sexy body and being the world's most inspirational parent to your children. If you can't do all of that, then you are just not good enough.

Success is never judged by what we achieve compared to other people it is measured by what we accomplish compared with what we are truly capable of. As the saying goes, if you judge the success of a fish by how well it can climb trees then you will always see failure. Regardless of your situation, physical mobility, background, race or gender. The choice is still the same, bounce back up and fight some more or stay down and be a victim. Nobody would have blamed Bethany Moore for staying down on the mat. She had been dealt the lowest, weakest hand anyone could get. She had the perfect excuse to quit, and yet she chose to play the hand she had been dealt. Bethany endured dozens of painful operations and defied the expert opinion that she would never make it to her teenage years. On her thirteenth birthday, she was recognized by a radio station as their local hero of the year. I was there at the Gala Dinner in her honor to watch her collect her award.

Today Bethany is 21 years old, my son and her still send each other a gift every year to celebrate their joint birthday. While many fully able-bodied people are still living with their parents and only just considering looking for a job, Bethany has her own specially adapted apartment and works full time as the receptionist for a large legal firm. If you think Beth landed that job out of sympathy, think again - she worked hard to prove that she was worth it and the extra cost the firm would have to make her workspace disability friendly. Bethany throws her all into that job, and she is a tremendous asset to the firm. Life dealt her a terrible hand so she could appreciate a lot of the things other people take for granted.

Yes, we are all born to win but in our unique way. As long as you are giving life your all and seeing the results you want, then this is the whole point of it all. However, I meet so many amazing people at my QUIT DRINKING BOOTCAMP events who know that they are nowhere near to full throttle. They recognize that they have got a sizable way through their lives and barely made it out of second gear. The first thing they want to know is why?

Lots of people remember their younger, braver days When anything seemed possible, and they had the energy to attack life like a warrior. But somewhere along the way stuff got real, too real and it started to feel a lot safer to stay under the radar. Other can't even imagine what it feels like to be that at peace with life. They grew up around people who told them they were not good enough and they believed it. Our environment is essential, especially in our formative years. We are like a sponge soaking up information. Just like a real sponge, if you drop us in a bucket of manure guess what our beliefs are likely to be made of?

There are five critical developmental stages in our life. These are crucial learning periods that establish who we are as a person, how we feel about ourselves and ultimately what we will achieve in life. The first time frame runs from birth to seven years old and is referred to as the Imprint Stage.

The Imprint Stage:

All our beliefs are created by experiencing new events that we have no prior data on or opinion about. Before the age of seven, we have so few points of reference that we will accept pretty much everything we are told as being a hard-wired fact. Especially if it comes from a trusted source such as the big friendly giants who feed, shelter and clothe us.

"What's that you say, there is a friendly old fat guy who sneaks down the chimney once a year a leaves us presents? Sure okay, seems fair enough".

When you are three years old, you don't touch the hot pan on the stove because you are stupid but rather because you do not have sufficient data to assess the action as a risk. However, if the adult who responds to your screams of pain then labels you as being stupid for touching the pan, it is entirely possible for the 'I am a stupid' belief to be born. You do not have the critical thinking to dismiss the statement and at an unconscious level accept it as a fact. Twenty years later you find yourself backing out of a career promotion because you conclude you are not intelligent enough to get the job. All beliefs are lies, even the good ones. It just that the 'good lies' serve you and the 'bad lies' don't.

We will talk about labels later in the book but what I mean by 'good' lies is... If you believe you are a fast runner that is a positive belief that serves you. However, if you want me to confirm that it is true, then the first question I have to ask you is 'compared to what'? Compared to Usain Bolt I am willing to bet you are somewhere between very average and awful. However, compared to me, sure you may very well be pretty fast. However, do you see the belief itself is entirely baseless and without supporting foundation? So when you tell yourself you are not good enough, the same premise must also hold. Not good enough compared to what? In the example, I made above about your first experience of touching a hot pan on a stove. You were labeled stupid by someone who was viewing the event from a different frame of reference. They had access to the data that steaming pans on stoves are a danger and you did not - this is not the definition of stupidity. It would be stupid if I stuck my finger in the electrical outlet to see what it felt like because I know full well the consequence of that action. Questioning your intelligence at that moment would be like a brain surgeon calling me stupid because I don't know how to operate on someone's head. You don't abuse your laptop and call it stupid before you install the software, do you?

I don't know of any under seven's who read my books. So I will forgive you for wondering why I am telling you this. Isn't it a bit like closing the stable door after the horse has bolted? A little, but there is also enormous value in this knowledge. Firstly, if you are a parent of young children be super aware that your words, deeds, and actions are being accepted as a hard fact. If you tell your child that they are 'very messy' you are laying the foundations for a lifetime of untidy habits. Conversely, if you want them to have the self-belief and inner peace that has always evaded you then tell them nice and early just how awesome and limitless they are.

The second important learning here is that all that negative garbage you say to yourself is most likely just that. You know what I am talking about, those moments naked in front of the mirror where you emotionally beat yourself up because your too fat, too short, don't have a big enough penis or your boobs are too small or the wrong shape. It's all 100% pure grade horse shit and nothing more. We are all living inside a bubble of our creation. If I tell myself that I am stupid, then it becomes true but (and it is a HUGE but) if I tell myself that I am super intelligent then that also becomes my reality - which world do you want to live in?

Wait, I can already hear some readers getting ready to object. "But, Craig if I am overweight and I tell myself that I am slim am I not just deluding myself"? First, I would answer by saying 'overweight, compared to what'? But more importantly, do you not see that like attracts like. If you firmly believe that you are slim and healthy, your subconscious will deliver this reality. Over eighty percent of the world's population lives in poverty because they BELIEVE that money is hard to come by or money is the root of all evil etc. Life is not something that happens to you it is something that is happening FOR you. The most exciting truth I share with people at QUIT DRINKING BOOTCAMP is that they are far more in control of life than they ever imagined. Everything that appears in your life is the physical representation of what is inside you. If you keep getting into unfulfilling relationships with the wrong man or woman, this has nothing to do with the quality of partners available in the world. The relationships that show up in your life are a direct reflection of how much you love yourself. I am sure you have heard the over quoted sentiment that *you can't love someone else until you first learn to love yourself first.* Sure, it sounds trite and a bit new age and hippy, but it's entirely accurate.

The Modeling Years

From ages seven to fourteen we enter a period of our development called The Modeling Years. We have started to interact with a more varied range of human beings socially. We are no longer only taking our references from our family, but instead, we begin to look to other people for knowledge. As such, we experience the pressure of social proof, conformity and the need to be accepted as a part of the group. There is still a vast amount of essential data missing from our personality, and we start to make the false assumption that other people know better than us. It is this reason that your teenage son or daughter goes crazy when you buy them the 'wrong' brand of sneaker or cell phone. In the modeling phase, we violently push away our uniqueness and desperately go looking for the approval of others. Perhaps this is why my daughter, Aoife, who has a wonderfully unusual Irish name, is known to all her friends (and on social media) as Eva. Of course, in a few years she will enjoy having an unusual name, but for the moment it is a hideous curse forced upon her by her unthinking parents.

In this developmental stage, we are not taking everything we hear as a fact; we can filter information now. However, we are more watching than listening to the world around us. Parent's your children are watching what you do and for the most part, ignoring what you say. I remember when I was a teenager my Dad would do all the things that would get my brother and I into trouble with our mother. He would put his feet up on the couch, leave his dirty dishes on the table and occasionally commit the cardinal sin of placing a drinking glass on the French polished dining table without a coaster. All of these acts committed by my Brother Mark or me were enough to send my mother into a rage. When we would point this out to my father, he would always reply with the same statement 'do what I say, not what I do.' That all sounds very good, but sadly it doesn't register in the mind of a modeling human being. We are mimicking the figures of authority around us because we believe this is how to get ahead. What we don't appreciate entirely at this point is the grown up's don't always act in a very mature way. There is an excellent reason why the children of alcoholics have a dramatically increased chance of also getting into trouble with alcoholism.

I am sure you can remember the cool kids from your school. The ones you thought were so insanely popular and if you could be more like them then... well insert any fantasy you can think of. Let me tell you; the scenes you remember from those times at school are a smokescreen. Those super cool kids were just as fragile on the inside as you may have been. They just found a different coping mechanism, an aggressive public display of defiance to conceal their fear. They almost certainly hadn't arrived at some amazing discovery or worked life out at an incredibly early age. I researched a few of the big names from my school days a few years ago. One of them works delivering pizza, another is onto his fourth marriage and the head honcho of the schoolyard, Andy, well he's in prison for robbing a Postal Office. What you observed and modeled back then was the same as what you see today, people doing the best they can with the resources they have - and no more than that.

The socialization Period

Between the ages of fourteen and twenty-one, we start to become aware that we are not just a child of our parents, but we are own men and women. We are unique human beings, here not to do what I parents tell us but to stride forth into the world and create our own destiny. This is why your loveable, communicative child becomes a teenager and mutates into a barely human monster who can only grunt the most basic of an answer. They lock themselves away in their room, disowning the family and appear to be misery personified. Until you see them laughing like crazy with their friends. It's hard not to take it personally, but in the socialization phase, we are discovering the world is a lot bigger and vastly more interesting than the bubble our parents reside in.

The Business Persona Phase

From twenty-one to thirty-five we are focused on our reason to be. We are choosing our career and progressing up the corporate ladder. During this period we are building beliefs, values and assumption about our ability to earn, progress and succeed in business or in the workplace. Despite being a fully mature adult human being it's surprising how much we still need to learn and just how much scope there is for change. I believe a great deal of marriages fail because the couple met and tied the knot before one or both of the parties really knew who they were. This is especially true for men. Guys in their twenties are often testosterone fueled demi gods who think they can conquer the world. By the time they reach thirty they are starting to realize that's not going to happen. The thirties can be a tricky decade for a lot of men, there is a lot to accept and adjust to. I don't believe we really know who we are until we hit our forties. Women generally (but not always) have got this life thing worked out a bit sooner than us.

Certainly in the case of my first marriage, I was nineteen years old when I met Denise, she was twenty-six at the time. I was still a baby, but I thought I was a man. By the time I hit thirty I had changed and developed so much that I was no longer the same man that walked down the aisle. Information is power but as the saying goes, with great power comes great responsibility. I believe you can expect to witness significant change in your personality every decade or so. If the life you aimed for and achieved is no longer rewarding then consider that this could be an explanation.

WHOSE FAULT IS YOUR DRINKING?

There is no arguing the fact; problems with alcohol can make you downright miserable. It can feel like being trapped inside an endless loop. You keep running, hoping against hope to find the exit but the same story just keeps repeating over and over. It all feels very much like the background scenery in a 'Scooby Doo' cartoon.

Society is a little bit twisted when it comes to alcohol addiction. People tend to approach addicted drinkers with pity, as though they are strange broken people. We don't treat smokers the same way. If someone told you they were addicted to nicotine, you would be highly unlikely to pour on the sympathy and declare how terrible it must be for them.

Because of this kink in our collective perception, it is very easy to feel sorry for ourselves. We can even avoid responsibility entirely by insisting that we have a disease called 'alcoholism'. Almost as though something unfortunate happened to us. However, this sort of pity party solves nothing and serves no purpose.

If you do join my online stop drinking program or attend a Quit Drinking Bootcamp, you will quickly discover that I am not the sort of therapist that is going to hold your hand and tell you how terrible it is for you.

Alcohol addiction is a miserable affliction, and we can choose to blame our parents, the marketing, the social conditioning or any number of explanations. But this sort of thinking and rationalizing will only delay and hinder your way out of the maze.

In the member's area of the Stop Drinking Expert, there are people who have been sober for years. There are also people who still can't go more than a day without drinking. If you ask me what the difference is between the two types of people, I would say: The sober people are willing to do all the things that the drinkers refuse to do.

People who are firmly committed to sobriety don't have excuses, only the drinkers do. Show me someone who is still drinking, and I guarantee you that they have a list of pre-prepared reasons why they can't stop yet! They will tell you that 'they are having a tough time at home/work at the moment,' 'they will just get Christmas out of the way,' 'as soon as the vacation is done and dusted' etc. The list of reasons to fail goes on and on.

Your journey to escaping alcoholism begins with a flat refusal to permit yourself to fail and taking 100% responsibility for the situation you find yourself in. Notice I did not use the word 'blame'. Blame in any situation is the pointless bleating of the ego and nothing more. Blame never serves any worthwhile purpose. NEVER!

For example, let's say your goal is to run the 4-minute mile. Unfortunately, during training one day you fall and break your leg. You may think that this is a really great reason to explain why you have failed to achieve your goal, and perhaps it is. But does using the excuse give you anything in it's place? You didn't run the 4-minute mile and an explanation is no substitute for that. You missed your target, suck it up and deal with it. Stop using excuses to justify your failure.

Remember the Rocky quote... winning has nothing to do with how hard you can hit. It's about how hard you can get hit and keep getting back up. When you come up with an excuse, you are choosing the stay down on the mat.

To become a happy sober person you take responsibility and develop an internal state of mind that takes ownership of the challenge. You must have a deep determination to deal with this problem no matter what is thrown at you. Not because someone else told you to or because you feel guilty about letting other people down but purely for the love of yourself.

Start by taking a pen and paper and sitting down alone. Write down every reason why you drinking alcohol. Common causes include:

- Because it helps me relax
- I need it to cope with my stressful life
- I can't sleep without a drink
- It's my only pleasure
- It helps me be more sociable

Keep writing until you have exhausted yourself. Keep scribbling until every single reason you have for drinking is down there on that piece of paper. Every sole reason to drink, even if it seems entirely logical, it is nothing but an illusion – including that list I just gave you. There is a reason why alcohol is the second most addictive substance on planet earth (just behind heroin). That is because it is exceptionally good at what it does and it is remarkably good at making all its traps and tricks look harmless and insignificant.

Alcohol hooks people in so slowly that you don't notice what is going on until it's too late. It's like falling into very thick and slow-moving quicksand. The sand is so thick that for a while you are completely unaware that you are sinking at all. It feels very much like you are standing firmly on solid ground, and so you keep on walking. Alcohol will let you get all the way out into the middle before it starts to pull you under. Just like being in real quicksand, kicking and screaming and blaming someone else for not warning you won't help you get out. All it will do is accelerate the speed at which you sink.

Wake up and smell the coffee! You got yourself into this loop and it is you who is going to get yourself out. I challenge you to learn the truth about every one of those reasons to drink that you noted down. Dissect them and tear them apart until you fully understand how the illusion is being performed. Then accept 100% responsibility for dealing with this addiction.

There is no magic bullet out there; there is no pill you can take to make this go away. There is a solution, but you can't buy it, because you already own it. It's inside you – your focus and commitment to get this poison out of your life at all costs is the secret to escaping the loop of alcohol addiction once and for all.

DOES ALCOHOL REALLY GIVE YOU CONFIDENCE?

Does drinking make you more confident? There is a really quick answer to this question…No! Alcohol really gives you stupidity, and there is a big difference between the two.

People believe that they feel more self-assured and confident when they have had a drink. There is even common parlance for it 'Dutch Courage'.

It's one of those expressions we use without giving much thought to where it came from. In numerous ways, the Dutch used to be Britain's dearest neighbors. From the rise of the United Provinces throughout the sovereignty of Queen Elizabeth I and up until the eclipse of the Netherlands as a major power in the Napoleonic conflicts. They were sometimes enemies but more usually co-religionist allies, significant trading associates and irregular provincial rivals. Even more than that a Dutchman, William, even went on to become king of England in 1689.

These connections between the two countries have forced the word 'Dutch' to appear repeatedly in the English language. Slang dictionaries have plenty of phrases such as 'going Dutch', 'Dutch auction', 'Dutch uncle' and of course 'Dutch Courage'.

'Dutch courage' has a pair of feasible origins. The first derives from the denigrating idea that Johnny Foreigner is a weaker chap that the strong and tough Englishman. Whether this bounder was cruising up the Medway or facing down the locals in the East Indies, he required a handful of drinks before a battle.

The second idea relates more directly to the use of a specific alcoholic beverage 'gin' to bolster one's 'confidence or bravery' in battle.

Gin in its contemporary form was reputedly invented by the Dutch physician Franz de le Boë in the 17th century. British troops fighting Louis XIV together with their allies in the Low Countries appreciated the calming influences of Dutch gin prior to heading into battle.

Whether it specifically referred to gin, 'Dutch courage' as an English colloquialism tended to mean using spirits, not just beer, to reinforce self-belief.

This all sounds very poetic and romantic, but the real story is less so. Front line soldiers in these sorts of battles were really nothing more than cannon fodder. They were considered the affordable and expendable casualties of war. They were the poor sods that would charge into the first and most gruesome line of defense while the opulent generals sat at a safe distance on handsome stallions looking on.

However, willingly charging toward your own gruesome dismemberment and eventual death doesn't so much need bravery or confidence. What's needed is a good dose of stupidity and poor decision-making. It just so happens that alcohol is perfect for inducing both these mental states in a person. Booze was the ultimate tool to manipulate men to die for their country.

Here's the hard reality. One of the reasons why alcohol is so good at what it does (successfully killing someone every minute of every day). Is because the very first thing the drug does is disable the section of the brain responsible for making sound decisions. This is why people find it so hard to have just one drink and then stop. While sober you have the seemingly unbreakable determination just to have one little drink. However, as soon as the drug plays its opening hand, you become as weak and vulnerable as a newborn baby.

This effect on the logic areas of the brain is also the reason why people become less risk averse after drinking.

Becoming less able to gauge risk does not make you confident it makes you stupid. So yes, you may have had the 'nerve' to approach the hot girl after you had had a drink but don't kid yourself that you were acting bravely or even more confidently.

No beautiful woman ever looks at a drunk man, who is clumsily trying to pick her up and thinks 'wow he is so confident.' The inebriated chump who firmly believes he can jump from one hotel balcony to the next is not being super confident.

There is no such thing as Dutch Courage. Alcohol makes you stupid. I would argue that in most of the occasions where alcohol is used for so-called Dutch Courage. For example, making a presentation at work, going for a job interview, talking to a man or woman you are attracted to, etc. Perhaps deliberately making yourself progressively less intelligent is about the worst possible choice you could make.

Don't you agree?

HOW DO YOU HAVE FUN WITHOUT ALCOHOL?

Drinkers can't imagine going to a party that doesn't feature alcohol. They will pre-decide that it will be boring and dull. Back when I was a drinker, I would have point blank refused to attend a party that didn't have alcohol. My ex-wife was friendly with a couple that hardly drank alcohol at all. Perhaps once a year we would be invited around for a meal. I would bitch and moan like a petulant child. Through the meal I would sip the water and continually glance at my watch. Fifteen years later when I look back, I can't remember anything about them, other than they stopped me drinking. They may have been the most lovely and amazing people who ever walked the earth – I will never know.

At the time I was 100% sure that I was right! You can't have fun without booze. However, the truth is it's not that alcohol makes a party, but rather drinkers of alcohol are miserable when they can't get access to their drug. So it's not the party that's dull, it's the addict – who only knows how to be sociable if they are able to engage in the consumption of their preferred drug.

At the height of my addiction, I couldn't even go to watch a movie without first planning how I could also drink at the same time. I would even sneak a bottle of whiskey into the movie theatre with me. I would order a big gulp coke and mix it with Scotch so I could sip at my drug for the entire duration of the movie. Pathetic.

Alcohol doesn't enable fun; it prevents it! This has been demonstrated to me this weekend in the most profound and hard-hitting way. I live in Cyprus these days and my grown-up children live in the United Kingdom. So I don't get to see them as often as I would like. This means that when we do spend time together, we want to make it count.

This weekend I flew to London to have a weekend in the city with my daughter. We had a fantastic time together; we went shopping, took in a west end show and spent serious quality time together. I am so grateful that alcohol is no longer present in my life to steal these moments from me.

Alcohol is a thief! It steals your money, your health, your relationships and worst of all – your time. I spent over £100,000 on, and while that is a crime, I can make more money! Time is the one thing you can never make more of.

If I were still drinking, this weekend would have been entirely different. Yes, I would have described it as 'more fun' but let me explain what a drinker's definition of 'more fun' really means.

We would have spent significantly less time doing what my daughter wanted to do. Lunch would have been in a pub and would have taken about 3 times as long. Afterward, I would feel a bit tired and suggest a lie down before we head out to see the show.

During the play, I would be thinking about the interval when I could have a drink. I would enjoy the show, as much as I could but it wouldn't have been the best part of the evening.

I would have woken up the next morning feeling terrible and full of guilt because the weekend was supposed to be about my daughter and yet again I made it about alcohol.

- In short, more fun means that I am here physically but not mentally.
- More fun means more selfish behavior from me.
- More fun means we will do less with the time we have.
- More fun means missing the whole point of the weekend.

How do you have fun without alcohol? That was the question that launched this chapter of the book, but it's almost impossible to answer. The whole premise that alcohol creates fun is a house built on sand. There are no foundations to support the hypotheses.

If you are skeptical, I can easily prove my theory to you. Just go to a party and be the only sober person there. You will be shocked at what you see unfold before your eyes.

Being the only sober person at a drunken party feels a little like being Neo in the Matrix. You are the only one aware that the 'crazy, fun world' being experienced by everyone else isn't real. The reality is much more sinister and scary than anyone is conscious of.

You will witnesses your intelligent and compassionate friends turning into bumbling, emotionally unstable zombies. You will sit with a bemused smile on your face, confused as to why everyone is laughing at a joke or incident that wasn't in the least bit funny. Slowly you will become aware that you are the only human being left in the room. Your friends have become nothing more than a bunch of chimpanzees on a sugar rush.

By the end of the night, many people will no longer have the brain power to speak, some will fall over and hurt themselves (much to the amusement of the other primates), and some will black out and have to be carried to bed.

The next morning all your friends will wake up feeling like they want to die before heading to Facebook to wax lyrical about 'what an amazing night we had.' Everything about alcohol appears to be a little bit insane when viewed with sober eyes.

Your friends will tell you that they had a fantastic night. But they will use words like 'slaughtered,' 'smashed,' 'wrecked' and 'wasted' to describe how they felt. They will look you straight in the eye and through their bloodshot, exhausted outlook say this to you with 100% conviction.

The question is not 'how do you have fun without alcohol,' the truth is drinkers don't understand what 'fun' is. Precisely the same way that people inside the Matrix refuse to accept that what they see isn't real.

You can't convince drinkers of this, so don't even try. You can't change other people; you can only change yourself and the way you respond to other people.

WE NEED TO TALK ABOUT BARRIE

This book exists partly because there is something wrong with our collective belief structures. From the day we set foot in primary school the corrupt lesson begins. We teach each other that in order to be acceptable you must be perfect, or as close to it as possible. You must wear the correct brand of clothing, you must be slim and attractive, you must be able to speak well and the list goes on. If it just so happens that you are born with a speech impediment or your parents can't afford to buy you the fashionable brand of sneakers that all your friends are wearing then you are going to have a tough time at school. You may be picked out and ridiculed because you do not fit the universally agreed upon definition of acceptable.

I don't care who you are, there are going to be emotionally traumatic events in your childhood. Because your brain is not sufficiently developed to deal with the horrendous pain that can be dished out by children, you will create coping mechanisms to help you survive. You may laugh off the abuse, you may retreat inside yourself and hide away from what is troubling you or you may even lash out and fight against the pain. The problem is we store all this erroneous information in our subconscious and we carry it with us through life. If during school you were

---

picked upon because the other kids said you had a big nose then it is likely you will be sensitive about this area of your anatomy when you grew up.

I was at a wedding a few weeks ago and I noticed one of the bridesmaids was particularly tall. She was easily six feet tall and as such towered over all the other bridesmaids and even her own husband. She was a strikingly beautiful woman, and she had the height to be a catwalk model. However, this stunning woman walked with hunched shoulders, almost curling herself into a ball to try and lose some height. Instead of embracing her height and loving that aspect of her being. She instead carries with her the scars of her youth. Perhaps at school she was ridiculed for being so tall, maybe they even gave her a cruel nickname. The result is, she goes through adult life viewing a unique aspect of her being as a negative, a draw back that makes her less attractive than other women. Her coping mechanism and internal programming is lying to her, she is seeing black as white.

We all have our demons, the things we worry about in the dead of the night. Perhaps you worry you are not intelligent enough, not articulate enough, slim enough, fit enough. We could go on and on with the list of nonsense that we allow to hold us back. Recently a simple Facebook post by one of my friends made me realize that we are all cursed with this problem. It also appears to me the more intelligent you are the more likely you are to suffer with this self-chastising behavior. In this book I am going to prove to you that all the nonsense you worry about is exactly that, nonsense! I will start this journey by telling your fortune, I am going to look into my crystal ball and make a statement about you that you will instantly agree sums you up perfectly.

'Everyone thinks you are so strong and secure but they don't

know that on the inside you sometimes feel like you can't cope.
You need a lot more love and support than they realize'.

Does that resonate with you? Well, I would expect it to, because it is a type of statement referred to as a 'Barnam Statement'. It is designed to feel as though it has been directed specifically at you but in fact it could be said to anyone and they would feel an attachment to it. Phineas Taylor ("P. T.") Barnum was an audacious circus pioneer and show-business impresario. He began his entertainment career in the 1830s by showcasing Joyce Heth, who claimed to be the 161-year-old nurse of George Washington. He briefly operated a small circus until it went bankrupt.

In 1841, he opened Barnum's American Museum in New York, which is considered to be the nation's first public museum of real importance. Barnum attracted customers by using various methods of creative advertising, such as hiring a man to lay a path of stray bricks for inquisitive folks to follow to his museum. His formula for financial success was to spend great sums of money to acquire an ever-changing display of strange exhibits for which the public would eagerly pay a small amount to see again and again. Some of his better-known humbugs included the Feejee Mermaid—bits of dried skin, hair, and scales passed off as a preserved sea nymph—and the Woolly Horse—a real horse with curly hair. Publicized as a horse "with his head where his tail should be," the animal was merely reversed in its stall.

Amongst his travelling band of circus entertainers, tricksters and snake oil salesmen he also had a team of 'fortune tellers' who would wow the public with their ability to sense things from people that nobody but there closest friends and family could possibly know. Of course they were doing nothing more that using statements and exclamations that Barnam himself had crafted to perfection. The statement i used above works so well because we all assume it is only us that have this inner weakness and doubt. The truth is we all suffer the same fate and nothing proves it better than what I saw on social media just a few days ago.

A Facebook post by a good friend of mine, Barrie Hodge, inspired me to write this book. Barrie is an amazing guy; I don't know anyone who doesn't love him to bits. You would have to look long and hard to find a bigger personality than this young Scottish guy. His antics even made it to the front page of the tabloid press one year when he was fired for streaking naked in front of the senior Labour Party politician Ed Milliband, who would later go on to become leader of the opposition. To save you wondering if I have used some authors poetic license or even just flat out exaggerated the story, let me quote you directly from the actual newspaper that covered the story.

A TOP radio DJ and his producer have been fired after a naked prank during an interview with Labour leader Ed Miliband.

Real Radio's Robin Galloway was caught by Labour aides trying to film nude Barrie Hodge in the background as Miliband chatted.

The Labour leader had his back to Hodge and saw

*nothing. David McCann, the journalist doing the inter-
view, was also completely unaware.*

*A Labour aide stepped in to block Galloway's view and officials later
called station bosses to demand they erase the video footage.*

*It is understood that Galloway, 48, who is famous for his pranks
on the radio, had meant to put the film on the Internet.*

*Last night, station insiders said that Galloway and
Hodge were carpeted after the incident at the station's Glasgow studios on October 28.*

They were suspended for a week and they were both sacked yesterday.

*It is understood the incident was viewed as "in-
decency in the workplace".*

*Sources stressed that no one else was involved and Gallo-
way's co-host Cat Harvey was not in the building.*

*A source said: "The station feel they have taken appropriate
action - the only action they felt they could take as a professional broadcaster - and the pair have been sacked.*

"It was felt the behavior had gone too far and could not be accepted."

*Last night, Miliband's office was in touch with Real Radio
to plead for the two to keep their jobs.*

*A Labour spokesman said: "We asked them to delete the
video and they were hugely apologetic.*

*"Ed was bemused more than anything else. All we did was
ask them not to show a video of a naked man."*

Miliband was said to be "horrified" to hear of the sackings.

A Real Radio spokeswoman said: "We can confirm a prank happened between Robin Galloway and his producer Barrie Hodge which got out of control.

"The station has taken appropriate action and regrettably both have been asked to leave the station.

"A letter of apology has been sent to the Labour Party. Further details regarding the Breakfast Show will be released in due course."

Without knowing the guy you may very well conclude that he is either a bit unstable or irrepressibly confident, perhaps even a bit of both. When you bring into the mix his warped and slightly twisted sense of humor I could sympathize with either assessment. I also know for a fact that Barrie himself would totally accept either pigeon hole you decided to ram him into.

Let me tell you about when I first met young Barrie Hodge. Back in 2009, I took over hosting the breakfast show for a large regional radio station in the North East of England and Barrie became my producer. Although on air he was never known by his real name. We referred to him as 'McTaggart', a made up and overly aggressive sounding Scottish name to accompany his Glasgow accent. We enjoyed playing up to the stereotype so much that when Barrie left and he was replaced by another Scottish guy called John McNally from Falkirk we decided that he would also be called 'McTaggart', the evil twin of former incarnation.

In my two decade long career in commercial radio, Barrie is the best radio producer I ever worked with. Barrie was always entirely focused on the show; he was always in a good mood and always thinking two steps ahead of any one else in the room. You may listen to morning show presenters on the radio and think 'wow what an easy job these guys have' and for the most part you are right. The biggest problem when you work the high profile breakfast show is one of having to play a character like an actor, while at the same time trying to appear like a real and authentic character in your own right.

Whether you are on the television or radio you always have to sound like you are in a fantastic mood. Nobody wants to wake up to some guy moaning and complaining. People have their own problems and they do not want to have to add your issues to their daily baggage. Radio for the most part is a make believe world where everything is always fine, the jokes are always funny and the music is never anything but amazing. The general public doesn't care that you just maxed out your credit card, had a row with your wife or buried the family dog. No matter how bad your mood is in real life, once the On Air light illuminates you are the happiest person on planet earth, it's the law!

I remember one morning pulling into the radio station car park. It was 5am and I was running late. There had been a hard frost overnight and at that early hour the parking lot had not been salted. I didn't know it at the time but there were patches of black ice all over the lot, this I discovered as I braked and felt my car slide into a wall. The impact split my boiling hot coffee into my lap and gouged a three-inch gash up two thirds of the side of my car. I walked into the radio station, a huge brown stain at the center of my crotch and swearing like a sailor. Nobody in their right mind would have approached me that morning any more than they would choose to tickle an angry bear who was busily chewing on a slab of freshly killed meat. But then many would say that Barrie has never been in his right mind, because he did a lot more than approach me. Within fifteen minutes he had not only distracted me from the crappy start to my day, he had me belly laughing so hard it hurt. You see, Barrie didn't see someone who was in an understandably shitty mood; he saw a very poor quality morning show approaching at a rapid pace. Unless he snapped me out of my funk, then the listeners to the radio station were going to tune 'this grumpy ass' out by the thousands.

Producer McTaggart would do whatever it took to make the show win, even at his own personal expense. He was the fall guy of the show and happy to be so, his fearlessness was awe inspiring not only for the listeners but also for me and the team in the studio. During our eighteen months working together I sent him out on Valentines Day in nothing but a thong, handing out roses to the ladies. We fed him the hottest curry on planet earth and listened to him scream like a little girl. We painted him head to toe in blue body paint and sent him out as a character called Blue Monday man, whose job it was to cheer up the people of the North East on cold and depressing Monday mornings. One morning we even pretended he had messed up our coffee order and so we locked him in the trunk of my car with my dirty gym kit for the entire duration of the show.

The producer of a radio or TV show is never the one to take the glory but often is the engine behind the success. I can tell you that the guys in front of the microphones, who took all the credit for the ratings, were in awe of Barrie. He seemed totally unshakable, with more confidence than most of us guys had in our little fingers. So when I saw the Facebook post by Barrie, the very same status update that you are about to hear for yourself, I was surprised to say the least. Firstly by the brave honesty he was displaying but also by the contrast between his public image and the stark reality of the real Barrie that he keeps hidden beneath his own unique veneer of super 'over the top' confidence.

Barrie gave me permission to post this exactly as it was written. Please forgive the coarse language in places; remember this was written to a closed audience of Barrie's closest friends and not the general public.

I don't usually post stuff like this but . . . I have a confession to make. I'm actually a really shy and quiet individual. Sure, I say inappropriate things a lot. I, more often than not, end up being the center of attention. You may think that is because I'm such a show off bastard. But the truth is I do that because it's how I deal with awkward social situations. I'm either too loud or too quiet; I never seem to get it just right. I can quite easily go for days without speaking to anyone, and be extremely happy about it. I guess that's why I enjoy spending so much time on my own, running for miles or disappearing on my bike.

I also suffer from crippling crises of confidence. I have painful panic attacks when I'm in a situation I can't control or can't figure out the eventual outcome. Few people see it as I keep that hidden. I try and give an air of confidence, which usually sees me through. But that veneer will fade away as soon as I'm on my own. I can easily breakdown as I become so overwhelmed with situations. Again, that's why I do the daft fitness things I do (such as running seven marathons in seven days). It's not to be fit. It's never been about that. It's a way for me to take control of something when I feel like everything else is falling apart. (Even when it actually isn't!)

Even though I always try to be optimistic, I can be incredibly pessimistic. Some people see me as the eternal optimist. Like when I've lost a job. All people see is me dusting myself off and getting back on it, like it hasn't really impacted me at all. The amount of messages I've got from people saying that has astounded me. Asking for advice on how to handle it when it happened to them. Truth is, you haven't seen me when I've sat in a dark room, shaking, not knowing how I'm going to get myself out of the mess I'm in. Trying to work out how I managed to fuck it up this time. Worrying that I'm going to end up homeless in some doorway!! (Ironic that I now work for a homeless charity!)

But there is one person who has seen those sides of me and has never flinched. Has never once been rocked by them and has never ran away when others have. And I'm so incredibly lucky to have her in my life.

She understands my need to get up today at 5:30am to get a train to the Lake District again after I broke my bike last month trying to cycle the toughest climbs she has to offer. She understands how fiercely competitive I am. Not with others, but with myself. She knows that I won't be able to rest until I've done it because, even though I can easily feel like a failure at times, one thing I will never allow myself to do is give in to anything unless I absolutely have to. She accepts how stupidly stubborn I am, even though it must infuriate her! That's why I'm on my way back to the lakes today.

She runs me baths after she sees how much I've broken my body doing these stupid things. I remember during that time I thought it would be a good idea to run seven marathons. She put together a survival kit with everything I would need to get through the week. So wonderfully thoughtful as I didn't even think I would need those things. (Stupid I know!) She supported that stupid decision as she knows it's one of the things that define who I am and accepts this side of me when many others wouldn't.

She sends me little messages through the day when she knows I'm really struggling, just to reassure me that, even if the worst possible thing happens, she will be by my side every step of the way. It *gives me the confidence to dust myself off, take a deep breath and carry on when all I want to do is lock myself in the bathroom and turn on all the taps to drown the noises from outside. (Something I would often do as a kid and have done a lot as an adult) And yesterday, when she saw I was panicking about my job for some weird reason, she gave me a cuddle and made me feel safe. Then, when I got home, she made me pizza, bought cheesecake and a new flavored vodka to try. (Espresso flavor. Very nice!) Just because she knows it would make me feel better. (And it did!)*

I'm not a soppy person. I'm not very romantic if the truth were told. I hate it when people write shit like this on Facebook normally. I've always been of the opinion if you want to tell your other half how much they mean to you then just tell them and don't spout it on your Facebook page. I've always seen that as a cry for help in a relationship. Like you're trying to justify your relationship to the world when perhaps you can't really justify it to yourself. But a dear friend of mine who I haven't seen in a while said to me recently that he didn't even know I was in a relationship. I have been for nearly six years!!! And that got me thinking. I should be shouting a lot more about her because I'm so proud of who she is and what she does. I often take her for granted because I can be very self absorbed. But, the truth is, she's my partner and we are a team. (And a bloody good one at that!) I don't really know what I would do if she wasn't with me. To use a cliché (and you know how much I hate clichés) I would literally be lost without her.

We have been through some tough and dark times together. But we have survived when it could easily have torn us apart. And I'm not daft enough not to know that there could be a time when we may look at one another and hate each other's guts. I'm under no illusions that the world won't throw other challenges at us. I have always been a realist and accept that sometimes things don't work out quite how you want them too. But I know how strong we are and how we have survived those dark times by working together. We will face whatever life has to throw at us as a team.

Kerry, you are a diamond. Thank you for being on my team and making me a better man every day I'm with you. I hope I can be half as good to you as you are to me and I hope to spend the rest of my life with you being the best I can for you

Wow, suddenly here is a guy who most people believe to have unshakable self-belief and now he is laid bare by his confession. Revealing that all the gregarious self-confidence, grit and determination comes not from what most people would assume to be inner strength but as Barrie is explaining, all this comes from what he perceives to be his inner weakness. When Barrie feels weak he reacts by forcing himself to appear strong. This is his shield, simply a coping mechanism for his self-doubt.

We all have coping mechanisms and of course they can be both negative as well as positive. Simple psychological tools, that we use to deal with our worries and doubts. As a rule we tend to default to the negative options, such as drugs and alcohol, anger and shyness because quite frankly they are a lot easier to do. Barrie copes by running programs that have the appearance of introducing positive side effects into his life, but that doesn't mean he is happy about it. He is still only 'coping' with his own internal discomfort, just the way that we all do.

What I am going to make you aware of in this book is the existence of a web of lies that infects and damages our lives from a very early point. There is an 'illusion of perfection' which has been manufactured and forced into our psyche by the media,

Hollywood and more recently the Internet. It reveals itself as the voice in your head that tells you that you are too fat, too short, not funny, not intelligent or any of the other million negative thoughts that the modern day thinking man and woman are subjected to by their own ego.

Teenage girls suffer horrendous bouts of depression and many go on to self-harm because they compare their bodies to those of the airbrushed, size zero women in glossy magazines. Boy's hide away, swallow their anger and become self destructive because none of the popular male role models out there appear to have acne and a greasy complexion like they do. Most of us take this destructive self-critiquing behavior right through our adult lives; many will carry this nonsense with them to the grave. It will prevent them reaching their full potential and deliver a life that was not quite all that it could have been.

Barrie's brave confession shows us that nobody, and I really do mean **nobody**, is safe from this insanity. I don't know you personally, but I do know that you are perfect just as you are. That may sound trite and a bit 1970's love and peace man, but I believe that if we would just stop beating ourselves up all the time we could achieve miracles. Barrie Hodge is the best radio producer I ever worked with in two decades in the professional media business. He achieved that position in my perception despite dealing with a head full of self-doubt and worry. Imagine what this guy could achieve if he knew for certain that he is perfect exactly as he is?

Now imagine what you could achieve if, before you did anything else, you loved your self first and accepted yourself as being perfect. Not in an arrogant way but in a loving act of compassion for your own being? That is what we will discover together through this book! There is an old saying that goes 'you will never be able to love anyone else properly until you learn to love yourself first'. I believe this to be true, but not just in the respect of relationships but these sentiments affect every aspect of your life. From your career, financial success, hobbies and pastimes through to your personal associations.

Are you ready to fall in love?

This book is a little unusual in that it starts at the end and not the beginning. When you leave your home to set off on a journey your focus needs to be on where you are going and not where you are. People rarely jump in their car and just start driving and only then decide where to go. Normally the vehicle is just a device to deliver your objective. As the song says, life is a journey and to unleash your full potential it is more important to know where you want to go rather than where you are right now. We start the same way at the QUIT DRINKING BOOTCAMP event and in this book you are reading now, at the outcome you want to achieve.

Next we will once and for all smash those limiting beliefs of yours that have been holding you back for so long. Then I will fit you with your new set of glasses. I am also a very vocal advocate that the level and ability of your communication skills is directly linked to your success to date. For that reason I am going to share with you some very powerful, advanced level communication secrets.

Before we get started I want you to be very honest with yourself about your life as it stands now. Below you will find something that looks like a pie chart. You will notice that it has some circles spreading outward from the middle that represent a rating of zero (at the center) to ten (at the edge) with ten being per-fectly happy and zero being downright miserable. Draw a line in each section that represents your current state in this area of your life. This will give you a visual indication of what needs work and where your focus should be as you begin this journey with me:

My Example:

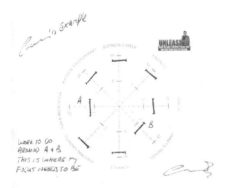

WORK TO DO
AROUND A + B
THIS IS WHERE MY
FOCUS NEEDS TO BE

SECTION TWO –
THE OUTCOME

FINDING YOUR PURPOSE

"Remembering that I'll be dead soon is the most important tool I've ever encountered to help me make the big choices in life.

Almost everything--all external expectations, all pride, all fear of embarrassment or failure - these things just fall away in the face of death, leaving only what is truly important.

Remembering that you are going to die is the best way I know to avoid the trap of thinking you have something to lose. You are already naked. There is no reason not to follow your heart.

No one wants to die. Even people who want to go to heaven don't want to die to get there. And yet, death is the destination we all share. No one has ever escaped it, and that is how it should be, because death is very likely the single best invention of life. It's life's change agent. It clears out the old to make way for the new", Steve Jobs

It's my deepest desire that with the help of this book is that you will discover for the first time in your life what you, honestly, truly want. That coupled with the practical application of the skills in this book to transform you into a shining beacon of happiness, peace, and purpose.

Of course, I don't know you personally, and the chances are good that we have never met. However, I believe that even without meeting you I already know two fundamental things about who you are, how you feel and what you want to happen next. If you are anything like me, you will have always had a nagging sensation that you are here to do something meaningful. You understand there is great potential inside of you and life has an essential mission for you. This sensation is what Nazi war camp survivor Victor Frankl described as the existential vacuum. It is a black hole in your being that is created by the failure to follow your heart and complete the task that you are here to do. This hole is painful and uncomfortable, it is always there at the background of your existence, and it won't go away until you fill it back up.

My brother in law once set up a business called SAHAFI. I asked him what the company does, and he replied 'anything.' Being rather confused by his answer I asked what the name meant, and he revealed that it was an acronym for 'See A Hole And Fill It.' This is an automatic response of human beings and we approach this internal vacuum with the same sticking plaster approach. We know there is a dull ache inside us created by this emptiness and so we desperately try to fill it up. Our favorite ways to do this are with material possessions, sex, drugs and alcohol and all other things earthly and physical. This universally pursued attempt to fill the hole is as effective as trying to fill a volcano by throwing matchsticks into it. Fruitless, pointless and a waste of time!

How many people do you know who give everything they have to climb the corporate ladder, to get onto the next pay scale to get the car with upgraded leather interiors?

How many people do you know choose where they live or the car they drive by comparing it to what their friends and neighbors have?

How many people do you know who max out their credit card so they can have a television at least two inches bigger than their friends have?

Does it ever make any of them happy, I mean a genuine sensation of peace and contentment with life? Maybe for a few days, even possibly for a few weeks but never (and I do mean never) for a lifetime. Money, cars, boats, houses, vacations, gadgets, technology and all this other 'stuff' we dream of owning are nothing more than matchsticks for the volcano. I don't know what your real purpose in life is, but I do know that it is not to own a great automobile or only ever stay in five-star hotels. People come to my QUIT DRINKING BOOTCAMP workshops to discover what they need to fill that vacuum inside themselves. When the hole is filled you are going to find that love, peace, happiness and joy floods into your life. All the things that you thought would bring happiness, such as money, sex, vacations, and abundance are not actually how you create happiness they are the result of being happy. The whole of the western world has got the whole puzzle the wrong way around. When you fill the vacuum, then all the good stuff will automatically flow into your life.

I am deadly serious about this; there is no limit to the amount of money, abundance, and love that can flow into your life just as soon as you start to travel in the direction you were always meant to follow. Let me ask you a question.

What do you want more than anything right now?

Whether that answer is physical or emotional, let me tell you that you can have it. But, only when you stop trying to force life to give it to you. Perhaps you want to meet the man or woman of your dreams. Maybe you have started to think that you will be on your own forever. Or are you one of those serial monogamists that go from one short and often dramatic relationship to the next, without ever finding that special person who you want to share the rest of your life with. Or perhaps you are the guy that never seems to get the break at work, missing out on promotions that you know you are more than capable of rising to?

Don't worry all these situations are just symptoms of the black hole inside you, pulling the exact opposite of what you want towards you. Once we fill this hole, the gravity of life will change. Just like flipping a magnet the opposite way around, suddenly what was once pulled into your path will now be repelled. And all the good stuff such as money, love, incredible relationships, success and peace will become drawn towards you.

Human nature causes us a little problem at times; we tend to be increasingly impatient and want the magic bullet cure for everything right now! We also tend to lean toward the incorrect assumption that happiness and success are a destination. That if we just 'earn enough money', 'live in the right neighborhood' or 'get the man or woman of our dreams' then we will arrive at nirvana. The universe is always expanding, and nothing in life is fixed in one place. The tree that stops growing new leaves is a dead tree. So, to assume that if we struggle hard enough, we can arrive at a place where all the bad stuff stops and all the good stuff becomes permanent is illogical nonsense.

One of my bestselling books is called 'Alcohol Lied to Me' and it has helped tens of thousands of people to escape the trap of alcohol addiction. The single biggest problem I have with this book is many people are so desperate to stop drinking that they flick through the book looking for the 'answer', the reason why the book gets five-star ratings. Often they are disappointed because there doesn't appear to be a magic bullet. People get back in control of their drinking by using this book, not by reading one magical concluding sentence on the last page but rather by walking a journey with me through the entire book. Just as in life, knowledge is absorbed through the trip we take. I am pretty sure that what you have learned since you left school massively outweighs the information your teachers tried to pour into your head by having you remember facts verbatim.

Life is about the journey, and I am here to tell you that you will never arrive at the end. This book is designed to profoundly change your life, just the way the knowledge I share in it changed mine. It took me forty years of struggling to swim upstream in life before I discovered the secrets in this book. I was an overweight; alcohol addicted angry man who never quite lived up to his potential. I suffered from depression, anxiety and low self-esteem for many many years. No matter how much money I earned, no matter how much I drank, no matter how many things I bought, the vacuum inside me just kept growing bigger and bigger.

Since I discovered the material, you are about to hear I have lost over sixty pounds in weight, quit drinking, given up my boring office job (to follow my dreams of being a full-time author) and moved to a beautiful island in the Mediterranean that boasts three hundred days of sunshine a year. I am forty-four years old, and these days I step out of my villa pick up my surfboard and spend the days on the beach with the woman of my dreams. Yes, I am insufferably annoying to be friends with on Facebook!

Now, it's highly probable that the life I just described doesn't sound all that amazing to you. Perhaps you hate the beach, and your dream environment is lost in the wilderness on some verdant hillside — just you and nature all alone and at one. We have a different vision of nirvana, and I am most certainly not here to enforce my view onto you. Neither am I here to boast, such an act of the ego would suggest that what I have is restricted to me alone. Quite the opposite is true, and I speak around the world on this subject merely to make the point that everything you desire is entirely achievable. But first, you have to stop living life safely inside your comfort zone and start to live your purpose in life.

So many people come to me and say 'Craig, that all sounds great and I want to start designing my own dream life. But how do I find my purpose? I have been looking everywhere, searching and hunting for it for so long but no matter where I look or what I do I can't find it'.

Do you know why they can't 'find' it? Because that's not how it works. You don't find your purpose, you decide on your purpose. Generally, there is not some divine intervention where you have an Isaac Newton moment sitting under an apple tree. Or you leap from the bath one-day crying 'Eureka, I found it.' Billions of people have died with their music still inside them because they sat around and waited for their life's mission to arrive in the mail one day. Every amazing idea, every giant corporation and even every small business venture started in the mind of one man or woman. None of them got given a magical blueprint to success or even a list of what to get started on first. They made a decision and then got to work. This decision does not need to include the precise route you are going to take or even the type of product or service you are going to create.

Your purpose may have nothing to do with career, business or money. It may be entirely motivated by serving humanity and helping others. Just don't get trapped into assuming you have to know every aspect of the plan before you can get started.

At the QUIT DRINKING BOOTCAMP events a lot of people struggle with this. They say to me, 'but I don't know what I want to do". I answer by reminding them to start at the end and describe how their life would look if everything were perfect. Once they have this utopia in their mind's eye, we can work backward from there. What does it take to get success, what would they be doing with their time to create a life so amazing as this? The answer may be that they would be running their own business but as it stands they don't have the skills and knowledge to do that. So, now they have the next step... learning to fill the gaps in their education. It takes a little vision and creativity to always start at the outcome instead of the start but hopefully you can see that if I ask you (for example) to make me a chocolate cake. Even if you don't know how to do it, you can do a little research, perhaps watch a few YouTube videos and find out. However, if I only tell you to go and make me something to eat and I will tell you if you got it right when I see it - your chances of success are limited.

When I started this journey to unlock my full potential, the outcome I had was pretty vague, but all the same, I felt excited whenever I thought about it. All I knew for sure was I wanted to be working for myself, only doing what I love, enjoying every minute of what I was doing and reaping a huge financial reward as the byproduct of that. The next thing I did was enroll in a professional photography course. Such an action never featured in any of my initial planning. I never set out to become a photographer and had not even thought about photography since I did it as a hobby at school. I believe by setting the outcome I presented my subconscious mind a challenge. The problem was to find something I LOVED to do, that didn't feel like work but I could run as a business. Something that would free me from the rat race and give me the ability to earn money while being creative. My subconscious sifted through billions of bits of data and came up with Photography. I didn't have the skills to be a professional but with a bit of time and effort that could be fixed. However, had I not ever set the outcome I think it's unlikely I would ever resuscitate a former hobby that had been sleeping for two decades.

If you are confused at this point thinking 'but you are not a photographer Craig.' Let me explain; photography was the bridge that got me out of the tedious nine to five job and daily three-hour commute. I never set an outcome to become a photographer; it was purely a link in the chain. It's a bit like learning to swim, the best course of action is rarely to jump straight into the deep end as far away from the edge as possible. The sensible course of action is to enter at the shallow end and progress deeper and deeper as your level of confidence and skill increases. I set up a photography business which I ran part-time for a year before I felt comfortable that it would provide an income sufficient that I could resign from my day job and start working for myself.

So, at this point in QUIT DRINKING BOOTCAMP I would point at one person and say 'What do you want'? For you to feel completely fulfilled and happy what does life have to look and feel like for you?

For some people the answer is short and to the point, for example 'I need to be in a deeply loving relationship earning enough to be living debt free'. Other people have a more materialistic view of perfection, which by the way is totally fine as well. There is nothing wrong with wanting money, as long as you know why you want it. If you tell me that you want to be rich I am only going to ask you 'and what will that get you'? It doesn't matter how weird and wonderful your dream life looks as long as it doesn't hurt anyone else and you have it clearly defined.

The story of Howard Hill, the famous archer, is a great help in explaining why it is so important to have powerful goals: Howard Hill was the world's most excellent archer; nobody was better with a bow and arrow than Howard. It's said that he never lost a single archery contest that he entered. He could shoot an arrow from 50 feet and hit the bulls-eye dead center. Then he could pull a second arrow out of his quiver and split the first one in half. This guy was terrific, exceptionally talented.

But I'm going to make you a promise here and now. If you spent 20 minutes alone with me coaching you, I could get you to beat Howard Hill in an archery competition. Oh, but of course we'd have to blindfold Howard first. Oh yes, and spin him around a bit, so he didn't know which way he was facing. Now you're probably thinking, well Craig, that's just stupid. How on earth do you expect Howard to hit a target he can't see? That's a good question. Here's another one. How do you plan to hit a target you don't even have?

You might be thinking 'well Craig this all seems a bit pointless, my goal is to do what I am passionate about and earn a living from it – that's why I bought your book dummy.' But you see, leaving the passengers behind, having an unstoppable life or an exceptional life is not a goal – it is the byproduct of a goal. In precisely the same way that money is not a goal, it is only what happens automatically when a plan comes together with passion and commitment.

If you examine the top one hundred self-made entrepreneurs in the world, you will find virtually none of them had a goal to get as much money as possible and become rich. These people will have become the best or first in their field and committed blood, sweat, and tears to their endeavors. While they were busy being passionate about their purpose in life, no matter what they did or how fast they spent it – the money just kept rolling in. I do believe that old Zig is right when he says you can get everything in life that you want if you will just help enough other people get what they want.

"Escaping the rat race is not a goal, quitting the day job is the byproduct of achieving a goal."

There is a reason why you haven't already taken the great leap into the unknown. Most people say they are afraid of what could go wrong. Fear can be useful, but you have to understand where it is coming from. If fear is coming from real indications that charging ahead in a particular direction is going to lead to financial ruin then fair enough – sit up and pay attention.

However, if the fear is being generated by lack of confidence, then an entirely different response is required. Spirit can't be built by setting a goal to be confident. If you came up to me and said 'Craig, show me how to be more confident,' I would say 'at what'? Do you want to make killer sales presentations, do you want to speak publically for a living or do you want to attract the man or woman of your dreams? Your goals need to be specific, measurable, achievable, relevant and timely (S.M.A.R.T). For example, I could set a goal that I am going to play professional football for the Niners.

But let's look and see if that fits In with our rules for goal setting. Sure it's specific and measurable – I would certainly know if I were out there on the field in the famous red and gold. However, is it achievable? I am a 44-year-old British man who has never played football in his life; I won't leave the house if it is raining and I don't particularly aspire to move any faster than the speed I get up to while walking my dogs in the Cyprus countryside. I don't care how passionate I get or how much positive self-talk I can muster, the chances of me achieving this goal are somewhere between slim and none. That doesn't mean it can't ever be a goal because I do believe anything is possible if you want it bad enough. But perhaps I need an intermediate aim to bridge the enormous gap between where I am now and where I want to be.

What I would like you to do is stop reading for ten minutes and grab a pen. Write down, as many goals as you can, there are no rules at this point – it doesn't matter whether your goals are big, small, crazy, impossible, childish or X-rated. If you want to be an astronaut, then write it down, if you're going to get the house painted by next summer write it down. But do try to think of things that you think you could do if you only had high enough confidence to do them.

Next, I want you to go back through your list of goals and give them a timeline. Make up a target date to achieve them by, make this a stretch so that it puts some pressure on you. There is no point having a small goal such as 'say hello to the cute receptionist at work' and then setting a ridiculous time to achieve this of 'within the next six months.' As you consider each goal ask you 'what is stopping me doing this right now or tomorrow'?

Now, take a separate piece of paper and write down the seven goals that are most achievable in the shortest period.

Example:

1. Join a gym and start getting fit – 1 Day
2. Start planning my escape from the Rat Race – 3 Days
3. Get to know Julia and ask her for a date – 2 weeks
4. Lose 10lbs – 6 weeks
5. Establish two new recurring revenue streams – 7 weeks
6. Raise money for charity skydive – 2 months
7. Do my first skydive – 3 months

Put this list somewhere where you will see it at least several times a day. I keep mine taped to the side of my computer monitor, but you could have it in the car, on your desk at work or even taped to the bathroom mirror. Make this a living-breathing document, as you achieve one goal replace it with another. I am reasonably confident that you could be alive for a thousand years and never struggle to find seven things you want to achieve. On my list at the moment are things like 'Take my son to watch the Forty-Niners play at the Levi Stadium, San Francisco – 6 months' and visit the 'World War II museums of Munich, Germany – 3 months'. Visit Australia for the first time.

The strange thing is, I have been doing this so long now that I am at the point where if I write it on the list I know it is going to happen. This makes writing something on the menu almost as exciting as the day it comes true.

But remember a piece of paper in and of itself is powerless. If you write a list of goals and do nothing then guess what will happen, that's right – nothing, zip, zero, nada! As Henry Ford said 'Nothing happens until something moves.' Even the biggest multinational companies such as Microsoft and Toyota started with the actions of just one man. One man or woman having an idea and deciding to take action forced companies that now employ hundreds of thousands of people around the world into reality. I firmly believe that everything happens for a reason and you ignore your intuition at your peril. So, I encourage you to take a few moments to write down your ultimate outcome. Close your eyes and visualize how your life will look and feel, step into the picture and absorb all the fantastic sensations. Spend as long as you need in this beautiful daydream and only when you are ready, open your eyes and grab a pen. Write down as precisely and potently as you can, who you are and what your life looks like. Make statements based in the present tense that start with 'I am', these are potent subliminal commands to your unconscious mind. It is important to focus on what you want rather than what you don't want. I am can sure you can see that stating 'I am fit, healthy and committed to enjoying a slender and toned body' is a much more powerful statement than 'I am not fat or lazy.'

My goal, vision, and values are so important to me that I have written them into a mantra that I say to myself with passion and energy every day, several times a day:

I am the millionaire changer of lives!

The powerful propagator of passion, peace, and purpose.

I am confident, engaging and unstoppable — a worldwide bestselling story of success.

I am no new age hippy by any stretch of the imagination. I believe my feet are firmly on the ground and I have a vibrant and healthy level of suspicion about most such claims. However, the one new thought concept that I have seen proven time and time again is that thoughts become things. Everything that appears in your life is a reflection of what's inside you and how much you love yourself. Many women complain to me that they can't find a good man, they tell me with great conviction that all men are cheats and only after one thing. Then they are surprised when this story keeps repeating. Equally, I have been bored stupid by the guys who tell me that women are only after their money and are out to take the very shirt from their backs. If that's what you believe, then you will see it reflected in every relationship you ever encounter. This concept holds for every area of your life. If you don't have enough money, love, sex, passion or purpose today, it's entirely linked to the level of your inner values, beliefs, and assumptions. The awesome news is, in the next chapter I am going to tell you exactly how to fix this.

For now, we still need to dig a little deeper into your outcome. You should have it written down in a concise but vivid statement by now. Next, I want you to ask yourself some compelling questions:

Environment:

When you are living this dream life where are you. For example if your dream is to become a world famous surfer, picking up awards and winning surfing tournaments all year around then living in the middle of a desert down, thousands of miles for the beach may not be an environment congruent with your goal. If your dream is to dedicate your life to looking after sick and injured animals and you currently live in a top floor studio apartment, then you can see your environment needs some focus. It's not all about location, it could be about your relationship or simply the use of space in your home, etc.

In all this process you need to think hard about this stuff and before you write anything down, ask yourself 'is this true or is it a limiting belief'? If you say that you can't set up a coffee shop in your neighborhood because there are too many already this could be true, but it's most likely to be a limiting belief. Think about it, for it to be true then it means nobody else on planet earth can come to your town, open a coffee shop and make a success of it. When you frame it like that, then it starts to look more like a limiting belief than a statement of fact, right?

Of course, if your dream is to set up a beachwear store and you live in the Antarctic then I don't think anyone could accuse you have can't do attitude.

Behavior

Next, ask yourself what you need to do differently to achieve your goal. Poor timekeeping is probably not a great behavior if career success is a big part of your objective. It could be that you need to start looking after your body a little better. Dumping the takeaways and junk food and hitting the gym on a regular basis. Take a look at the routines of some of the world's most successful people, and you will notice some striking similarities. Richard Branson works out for several hours every day, not because he wants to or that he hasn't got anything better to do with his time but because he has identified that looking after his health is an essential ingredient in achieving his goals.

I know someone who's ultimate dream is to become a million-aire health coach. His goal is so specific that he only wants to work with business CEO's and industry leaders at a rate of $10,000 a day. The problem at the moment is he still drinks alcohol on a daily basis. He needs to ask himself if that is the behavior that will lead him to the outcome he is so passionate about living.

Capabilities

What do you need to learn to make your dream become a reality? When I decided to become a photographer, I began passionately training to learn the skills required to do a fantastic job for my clients. Of course, anyone can buy an expensive camera on Amazon but does that make you a photographer?

Values & Beliefs

Next, examine what values and beliefs are essential to the success of your outcome. If you believe that children are awesome little bundles of pure potential and your goal is to be the best provider of childcare in your state then that's a perfect match. However, there may be some areas of your life that need some work.

A lot of the values and beliefs that you have that don't serve you are being generated by fear. A little later we will talk about something I call Fear Technology. It's the most powerful technique for destroying fear you will ever find.

When I decided that my future was not just about writing books and recording audiobooks in comfy studios, but I wanted to get out there and speak to people I had to address some of my own erroneous beliefs and values. I used to really struggle with small talk and I would avoid it at all costs, labeling it as a waste of my time and pointless. However, I understood that if I was serious about living my dream, this was a fear-based belief that was going to do nothing but hold me back.

Identity and vision

Finally, ask yourself what sort of person you are, how do you see yourself, what do you stand for and how do other people see you. If you believe you are a super friendly, kind and loving person but everyone else says you are asshole maybe you need to spend a little time on this area.

I always remind my Stop Drinking Expert members that if you lie down with dogs you will get up with fleas. By that I mean if you quit drinking but continue to hang around with your drunken friends in the same environment as before then you may have raised your standards in one respect, but you will see be seen in the same way by most other people. It's challenging for the newly sober to run an inventory of their lives in this way but as the saying goes, it doesn't matter how convinced you are that you don't want a haircut. If you sit in a barber's shop long enough, you will end up getting one.

10X YOUR GOALS

"You are capable of more than you know. Choose a goal that seems right for you and strive to be the best, however hard the path. Aim high. Behave honorably. Prepare to be alone at times, and to endure failure. Persist! The world needs all you can give", E. O. Wilson

QUIT DRINKING BOOTCAMP audience members go big, or they go home. When you dream, you should dream big. Don't just plant a tree; plant an orchard in your imagination. What you sow in life is also what you reap.

Are you living 10X?

"Being cautious needs you to act warily, and there is no chance that you will ever reach 10X activity levels by being so careful.", Grant Cardone

Examine your objectives for this year. Chances are good; they demonstrate at least some fearful reasoning and less-than-creative thinking. I have no doubt (without even meeting you) that your targets are much less demanding than you can deal with. Trust me on this; you are a higher manifestation power than you currently understand. You can deal with much more than you believe.

You can change and adjust to just about anything life throws at you.

As an illustration, if your target this year is to make $50,000, I challenge you to improve that intention to $500,000.

That may seem insane but let me ask you, would you rather hit a target of $50,000 or fall short of a target of $500,000. Even if you fall short by 80% of your outrageous goal you still have double what you would have had if you had pursued the smaller and much more comfortable aspiration.

When you 10X your objectives, you will be compelled to handle your aspiration in non-conventional and ingenious methods. The conventional strategy does not work with 10X planning.

Not only does your consciousness have to develop in what you prepare and pursue, but your day-to-day energy has to transform too. Equally, as individuals undervalue their potential, they also undervalue how much work and time something will take. Therefore, a lot of people are often late for meetings and fail to complete ventures they start.

Instead of insisting on and assuming you will always have perfect conditions, prepare for adversity. As opposed to undervaluing just how much effort and time a specific thing will take, overestimate those factors. Put way more hard work into your objectives than you presume really needed to get there.

If you're going to think 10X, you need to also invest 10X personal energy. Without having invested the hard work, it does not matter how "outrageous" your goals are. As soon as your energy, effort and actions compliment (and surpass) your objectives, your Unstoppable dreams will swiftly come true.

Call to action:

" How can you accomplish your TEN-year plan in the next six months?", Peter Thiel, co-founder of Paypal

Examine your objectives, how can you 10X them? How can you constrict your focus? Or get inventive? Or approach things in different ways to achieve unorthodox outcomes?

Ready to get inventive and get daring?

Go "All in"

" As soon as you decide, the cosmos colludes to make it come about.", Ralph Waldo Emerson

Individuals are often scared of real responsibility. We 'd rather keep our options open than commit 100% to an endeavor. We 'd rather vary our financial investments to reduce risk.

But if you intend to go big, you have to put all your eggs in one basket. It sound's scary, but it's far more straightforward and less precarious to concentrate on just one basket than many baskets. And yes, of course, failing is a risk but are you here to linger in the 80% or are you here to step out of the congestion at the bottom of the mountain and join us at the top?

The moment you figure out what you want, over-commit to that project. Go all in. Pass your point of no return. When you do this, you'll discover the genuine implication of security and safety, which can only originate from within.

Once your safety and security are apparently coming from inside yourself, instead of anything outside of you (like a consistent salary, medical insurance, or pension plan), you'll see yourself in an entirely new light. Your belief and faith in yourself and your capabilities will drastically intensify.

The challenges that at one time held you back will end up being devices to push you ever onward. Your peripheral environment will complement your inner aspirations.

Call to action:

How you set the game up is more crucial than whether you are playing in the game. To succeed before you play, make daring decisions and vows of what you will achieve in advance. Public pledges that demand you to perform to an exceptional degree.

Eighteen months before my business crossed the million-dollar point I told my closest friend and family that my goal was to be a millionaire within the next two years. I stated as a fact that within one year I would be comfortably past my first half million and I would reach my full goal shortly after that. Yes, of course, many of them told me I was unrealistic, my father told me to stop being so bloody ridiculous.

But you see, I wasn't asking their permission, seeking validation or even testing the feasibility of my dreams. I was stating my intention publically. I was expressing the facts as I saw them. My goal was so clear, so sharp and so real in my mind's eye that it felt impossible for me to consider it not happening.

Like preparation, your energy and implementation should complement (and surpass) your decisions and pledges.

I encourage you to get clear in your mind about what you are going to achieve. Make your objectives public and commit big to your dreams.

SECTION THREE
– DESTROYING
LIMITING BELIEFS

EMPTY NEST SYNDROME

This book is designed to be a complete life overhaul. The focus is not on stopping drinking – I am assuming you have already done that using my other books and courses. However, I will occasionally pause the journey to talk about a particular challenge or obstacle.

As I travel the world with my Quit Drinking Bootcamp, I have lost count of the number of amazing mom's and dad's I have met who are suffering from something called Empty Nest Syndrome. It's something that doesn't get a whole lot of attention in the media, but it is a powerfully painful thing to deal with for many people. Painful enough to send then reaching for a sedative to make it go away.

Change is challenging for most individuals, and it's unavoidable in life. It may be particularly tricky, however, for a mom or dad all of a sudden coping with an empty house, that moment in life when their last teenager or grown-up child finally leaves home to set out on her own. For many moms and dads, the freshly abandoned home ushers in the liberty to discover their own daily lives more intensely. Others parents, having said that, are incredibly saddened by the experience of sending those not-so-little-anymore boys and girls off into the world. The psychological ache can be considerable enough to set off (or aggravate) a dependence on drinking, resulting in misuse or addiction, and a necessity for addiction therapy.

What Is Empty Nest Syndrome

Empty nest syndrome happens when a mom or dad experiences deep and long term unhappiness, solitude, or grief when a child (typically their last child) vacates the home for the very first time. Even though it's not a medically recognized disorder, its manifestations are very genuine. Sometimes, the effect is severe. Empty nesters can battle with serious despair or unhappiness over the loss of their son or daughters' continuous presence in the house. The quiet from bedrooms once full of happiness, gossip, and giggling is unbearably loud. Challenging feelings vary from apathy and boredom to tearfulness and melancholy. For those whose lives orbited completely around their kids, whose whole sense of worth and value originated from being needed as a mother or father, the loss may be overpowering.

Although most imagine an empty nester as the mom who's sobbing at the door as her son or daughter drives away, analysis has revealed that dads are also profoundly affected by a freshly vacant household. In a report carried out by Doctor Helen DeVries, the mothers had a less challenging time than anticipated when their kids left home. Instead, they were already considering the next phase of their lives. A lot of the dads, however, mentioned being psychologically caught off guard for the loss. They were also more prone to feel remorse regarding missed opportunities and a shortage of quality time with their kids when they had the chance.

Empty nest syndrome may result in alcoholism and dependency if a parent relies on drinking as a way of easing undesirable feelings. Alcohol may supply a short-term release, numbing unpleasant feelings or mitigating stress and anxiety about the future. Sadly, though, the desired benefits are short-lived. Not only that, if alcohol consumption becomes a routine activity, increasingly more will be needed to get the same impact. As problem drinking takes hold, shifts occur within both the physical body and the brain, affecting everything from how a person reasons to the way his/her major organs perform.

Empty nest syndrome isn't always the only root cause of a drinking problem that forms or becomes worse after a child leaves home. Numerous other variables can also raise the danger that an aging mom or dad will have a problem with alcoholism.

While the unfavorable emotions of an empty nest can impact any parent or caregiver, some people are more susceptible to alcoholism. For instance, clinical depression is a significant risk variable for problem drinking and dependency. If there's a history of depression, it can result in a raised danger of excessive alcohol usage. This susceptibility is particularly elevated throughout significant life modifications, like a grown-up son or daughter leaving home.

Dynamics within the household might move unfavorably too. For instance, caring for little ones might be the single most significant activity that a husband and wife carry out together. What happens when that task they've devoted so much time focusing on is effectively gone? For the very first time in decades, two individuals can all of a sudden end up a "husband and wife" rather than "mom and dads." It's not unusual for one or both partners to feel that the other has changed since the relationship started several years previously. Relationship problems can push an already sensitive individual to look for alleviation in drinking.

Monetary concerns can also intensify the unfavorable feelings of an empty nest mom or dad. Lots of parents stress over shelling out for their son or daughter's college expenses, including university tuition and living expenses. With the skyrocketing costs of university, this amount can rapidly get to $35,000 or more, only for a four-year diploma. Retirement is typically not far around the bend during the time kids become grownups. For moms and dads who have been engulfed by the duty of caring for a family, the strain of not having accumulated adequate pension funds can add additional pressure too.

Along with the variables discussed above, the empty nest commonly accompanies a considerable time of life for lots of moms and dads. Moms might be experiencing perimenopause or menopause, which could be taxing per se. Hormonal changes and shifts can quickly create chaos with feelings, and even set off a spell of clinical depression. Lots of moms and dads are also taking care of other significant life adjustments, like looking after an elderly parent or grieving the loss of one.

There's no doubt that this period of life can leave many mothers and fathers feeling alone, anxious, restless, uneasy, or upset. When all these adjustments and hostile feelings appear to stack one on top of the other, a drinking problem can quickly build in susceptible or predisposed folks. Addiction therapy can become essential to turn things around.

Therapy for Drinking & Empty Nest Syndrome

Empty nest syndrome is not rare, but self-medicating with alcohol is never a remedy. If you or somebody you love is coping with feelings of unhappiness, stress, and anxiety, or sadness by drinking heavily, it's time to reach out for help.

What I am about to say about empty nest syndrome also applies to every other problem people are using alcohol to try and fix. If you lose something you love from your daily life you absolutely must replace it with something. If you leave a vacuum behind it will grow and deepen. A little later in the book, we are going to talk about finding your purpose - at Bootcamp, when I raise this subject the empty nesters say 'but I had already found my purpose, and I lost it, so what do I do now'?

My answer is always the same; all that love, compassion and patience that made you a fantastic parent is still there inside you. The first thing you have to do is see that beautiful side of your personality as a huge benefit and something of significant value. Caring, protecting and nurturing other human being gave you a sense of purpose and let's be honest, it made you happy. So why have you stopped?

Is it not true that there are millions of people and animals in this world who are desperate for someone to care. You have a wonderful gift, you are filled to the brim with love and just because the people you have lavished that gift on for a couple of decades have moved away does not mean there is nowhere for it go anymore. The pain you feel in the moment is a signal that you are not doing what you are here to do. You can try and silence it with alcohol but you already know how that worked out, or you can stop damming the river and let the love flow once again.

V is for Victim

> *"Let me tell you something you already know. The world ain't all sunshine and rainbows. It's a very mean and nasty place, and I don't care how tough you are, it will beat you to your knees and keep you there permanently if you let it. You, me, or nobody is gonna hit as hard as life.*

> *"But it ain't about how hard you hit. It's about how hard you can get hit and keep moving forward; how much you can take and keep moving forward. That's how winning is done! Now, if you know what you're worth, then go out and get what you're worth. But you gotta be willing to take the hits, and not pointing fingers saying you ain't where you wanna be because of him, or her, or anybody. Cowards do that and that ain't you. You're better than that!*

> *"I'm always gonna love you, no matter what. No matter what happens. You're my son and you're my blood. You're the best thing in my life. But until you start believing in yourself, you ain't gonna have a life." - Rocky Balboa*

I want to tell you about Katie, I am sure you know her already, perhaps not the same Katie, but certainly 'a Katie.' Poor Katie drew a bad hand in life; she didn't do great at school because, as she tells the story, the teachers were idiots. She always dreamed of a cool apartment overlooking the sea, with a little dog called Jack. Unfortunately, because her boss is an asshole she has to rent a crummy little studio apartment in a rough part of town, and since the landlord is a total douche and doesn't allow pets, she is not even allowed to have a dog.

Talk to Katie yourself, and she will tell you how unfair life is and how she deserves so much more. Way more than 'so and so,' 'whose it,' or 'what's her name,' yet they have everything she wants. She will tell you that nobody understands her and that all her friends are two-faced bitches who are out to cause as much trouble as possible.

Is it conceivable that Katie just got an unlucky break in life? Is there any chance that she is correct in her assessment? Let's put it this way. Not a chance! Katie is a victim, and these victims are everywhere—we can't move for them. These are the people that believe life owes them something, and they often spend an entire lifetime furious that the neighbor got yet another new car, or so and so got promoted at work.

Victims not only suck the energy out of their own lives but do the same for anyone who comes close enough to get caught up in their vortex of doom. I call them mood Hoovers and I am almost certain you can think of at least a few people who fit perfectly into this description. Let's first talk about how you deal with this trait in other people, and then I want you to look within. We'll have a little honesty session and examine areas of your life where you may have adopted the roll of victim because it is easier than facing the hard truth.

How do you help a victim? The short answer? You can't because they don't want to be helped. They like being the victim; it gives them a convenient explanation as to why their life blows chunks. On their deathbed you could ask them 'why didn't you live the life you were truly capable of,' and they will have enough plausible deniability to stubbornly point at something or someone and say 'because of that.' All the time they are pointing a finger of blame at everything and everyone else around them, they are blissfully unaware that they have three fingers pointed right back at them. It is frustrating to care about this type of a victim because you can see the huge untapped potential in them, but they cannot. When they look in the mirror, all they see is someone who has been badly treated by life.

If they are a friend or family member, perhaps even your son or daughter, you will desperately try to help them see the truth, but in my experience all you will end up doing is expending vast amounts of time, money and energy to get precisely nowhere with them. The harsh reality is this; we are all divine creations. We each have a fragment of God embedded within us, and we all have the power to perform our own miracles. If we take decisive action and flow with the universe instead of kicking violently trying to go back up stream, we can manifest breathtakingly amazing lives for ourselves. Victims have this power too, but they choose to ignore it.

How to spot a victim

Victims have reasons, lots of them and often they seem like entirely logical and plausible explanations.

- I am ill because the doctor gave me the wrong medicine.
- I am poor because my boss is a jerk.
- I got fired because I am a woman.
- I became redundant because I am black.
- They won't employ me because I am white.
- I can't quit drinking because it's the only pleasure I have left.
- I am too stressed to stop smoking.

The list goes on and on, and all of it is 100% bullshit. There are four certainties in this life. You will be born, you will die, and in between, you will pay taxes and life will repeatedly knock you down. As Rocky Balboa says, 'Ain't nothing going to hit as hard as life.' Getting knocked down is not bad luck any more than turning on the tap and getting water could be considered good luck. Life is getting knocked down; the choice is getting back up again, looking it in the eye and saying 'is that all you got, hit me again, but this time put some effort into it!' The reason you can't help the victims is because when they do get knocked down, they love it. It gives them what they want, an excuse not to get back up again, and proves the point they've been trying to make all along. They are like boxers who are too tired to keep fighting and are hoping for one decent punch so they can fall with dignity and stay the hell down until the referee counts ten.

Exercise

Stop reading for ten minutes and think about the victims in your life. Ask yourself who they are, how long they have been there and most importantly, how much time you are spending trying to make them feel better. Which, in case you hadn't noticed, is like trying to push oil uphill. Once you are clear about who these people are, I want you to make a conscious decision to spend less and less time in their company–until they are no longer a part of your life. That's right; I am asking you to fire the mood Hoovers in your life. You can't help them, and they are not helping you, so it's time for them to go. There is a way to help, but it is almost certainly not what you are doing at the moment. If dumping them out of your life is not possible, or you are not comfortable doing that, then at least reduce the amount of time you spend with them.

But wait... what if you are the victim?

Are you a victim? This is a pretty easy question to answer; think of something in your life that you are not happy with. For example, you need more money. Now with that problem in mind, explain to yourself why this is your current situation. If you find you have answers and excuses readily available (such as because my boss keeps overlooking me for promotion), then you are operating in a victim mindset around this topic. If your response is more positive and places responsibility on your shoulders. Then you are in an abundance mindset (for example—I took a pay cut to change the direction of my career, but I know if I give this new job 100% I am going to earn far more than I would have in the old role).

Having an abundance mindset always starts with you taking 100% responsibility. Let me give you an example from my own life. In 2007, I bought a villa in Cyprus. I didn't know it at the time, but I was investing at possibly the worst time in the last century. Property prices were hugely overinflated, and there was a mad rush of eager buyers trying to get in on what was being touted as a gold rush. Realtors promised anyone who would listen that you could easily double your money within a few short years. I had always wanted to live in the sunshine by the sea, so I went all in. Three months after I collected the keys to my property the Lehman Brothers collapsed, and the whole western world went into a financial meltdown.

Overnight, my property lost 40% of its value, but that was irrelevant, as the whole market had evaporated. Due to a concrete explosion over the past few years, the tiny island of Cyprus found itself with thousands and thousands of new build property and absolutely no buyers to be seen. To make matters worse, I had taken a mortgage in Swiss francs on the advice of the bank. Because Switzerland was considered a safe haven outside the crashing dollar, pound, and euro, their currency value went through the roof. My mortgage payments tripled overnight.

Whose fault is this disastrous investment? The victim would say it's the realtor for advising me badly; it's the bank for selling me a volatile product or any other number of villains that could be pointed at and labeled as the 'fault' behind this mess. But at the point where you create an excuse, you become a reaction to life. You are a passenger who is responding to the events of life that are thrust upon you. Conversely, when you accept 100% responsibility for the events around you, then you are in the driver's seat. Let me tell you when you are alone in a runaway car, the last place you want to be sitting is in the passenger seat.

There were times when I believed this investment alone was going to be the first domino in my financial ruin. I considered handing the keys back to the bank many times and I have had more sleepless nights about it than I can count. However, a decade later I am sitting here in that same house writing. I paid the mortgage off twenty years early and it is the place on earth I truly call home. Downstairs my little zoo of rescue animals is cuddled up together and in the bedroom my beautiful, amazing wife is sleeping, oblivious that she only has 20 minutes of sleep left before I will slip back under the covers and gently wake her up for work.

There is no failure in life, only feedback. Remember that!

Exercise

Stop reading and grab a pen. I want you to write down every negative thing in your life that you believe is there because someone else put it there. Then next to each bullet point I want you to come up with a new and positive spin that gives you 100% responsibility for the event. Now wait, let me be clear. There is a huge difference between blame and responsibility. I am not asking you to take the blame for the day you got mugged in broad daylight or the night your car got stolen. Fault and blame are pointless actions of the ego, blaming the mugger for attacking you doesn't undo the act of violence that occurred.

What I want you to do here is accept the situation as being a part of your life. You may not have chosen to have it happen, but for whatever reason it did. It's a part of you, and that means you are the only person who can heal it within yourself. Make peace with it and try to give yourself a point of view that does precisely zero finger pointing and has a high expectation that a positive outcome will result.

These exercises are very easily skipped and forgotten about, but please try to do them because they make a huge difference to the speed at which you can bring positive change into your life.

DESTROYING YOUR LIMITING BELIEFS

"As I walked out the door toward the gate that would lead to my free-dom, I knew if I didn't leave my bitterness and hatred behind, I'd still be in prison." - Nelson Mandela

I am sure you have at least heard of the book by Rhonda Byrne called 'The Secret' even if you have not read it. Also, you will either believe in the Law of Attraction, abjectly refute it or remain open-minded enough to wait and see. The law of attraction is not a new concept, and Rhonda Byrne did not invent it. It is a principle of manifestation that has been speculated upon for thousands of years. Books like The Secret simply brought a dumbed down version of it into the mainstream spotlight.

The Law of Attraction states that what you think about 'most of the time' and what you believe at a subconscious level with manifest into your life. Ergo, if you believe you look fat, then you are directly making the very thing you don't want appear in your life. Conversely, if you fundamentally think that you are a highly successful and wealthy individual, then this reality becomes solid too. You probably won't be surprised, as I have already stated that I firmly believe thoughts become things, I am an enthusiastic user of the Laws of Attraction to direct and enhance my life. I will go further than that and claim that I directly used the law of attraction to transform my life completely. It was the lowest point in my life. I was depressed, broke, alcoholic and out of options. I had been fired from a job for the first time in my life, and my marriage was collapsing around me to add to the misery. I started to study the law of attraction because I had run out of any other options. I will spare you the details because this is not a book on how to manifest your destiny. Over the space of six months I changed my beliefs, I change my thinking, and I stop resisting life. The result was a total reversal of my situation. Within half a year I took myself from rock bottom to financial freedom, career success, 57lbs of weight loss, insanely good health, and fitness and a whole lot more besides.

That's all gravy! However, I do understand that not everyone believes in this sort of stuff. If I explained this to my own father, he would tell me I had gone soft in the head, and I need to see a shrink. Had I not witnessed it for myself I would tend to agree with him. The fantastic news is since I first started writing about the Law of Attraction I have discovered a logical, scientific explanation for why it works. This means I am in a unique position here to tell you about the principles and then prove it to you with fact. So, if you are the sort of person who is more likely to side with my father than Rhonda Byrne and her like, stay with me through the new age , and I will reward you with a massive slab of logic.

The Law of Attraction states that within you there is a source of manifestation power that is capable of creating an abundance of anything you desire. This fantastic and divine ray gun will amplify and magnify whatever you point it at. But here's the catch, there is no instruction manual and no safety switch. It doesn't warn you before you fire it and if you choose to point it at poverty that is exactly what you will get more of. So, you might think 'why don't people just make sure they point it at good things'? It's a good observation, but it's not quite as simple as it appears. Noticing that your neighbor has a better car than you and deciding you want a better car as a result of this does not point the gun at manifesting an automobile. Instead, the gun gets aimed at your jealousy and scarcity mindset. Rather than pulling up on your drive a few days later in your new Mercedes you get more and more angry as you watch your neighbor get a pool installed and head off on his third vacation of the year.

The main reason we cast the wrong spells and point the magic ray gun at the opposite of what we want is we give control of the device to the voice that shouts the loudest. Do you remember being a small child at school when the teacher asked a question, and you realized you knew the answer? Do you remember how high in the air you shoved your hand? So high that you had to use your other hand to support it and keep it defying gravity up there! Inside us, two elements direct the flow of our life: the soul (or subconscious if you would rather stay clear of any religious undertones) and the conscious or ego.

Humanity has a problem and quite a significant one; we perceive the ego to be a gift when in reality it is a curse. We believe the ego to be a unique facet of our individuality that gives us independence and character. The ego, in reality, is a fragment of our being that is quite frankly insane. Such is the insanity that it has even managed to convince us that bad is good and vice versa.

When we talk about the ego, most people assume we are referring to one specific type of selfish behavior. However, the ego is so much more than that narrow band of negative patterns and yet that doesn't mean there is a good side to it, no aspect of the ego can be viewed in any positive light or considered an advantage to the human existence. The ego is the insane part of our physiological , and absolutely nobody is free of it, not even the most enlightened being. We all have different strengths of ego and ergo according to levels of insanity that present themselves in a myriad of different ways that we might label as character traits or personality.

The first thing you should know of this part of you is that the ego cannot ever be satisfied, it can only ever be sedated temporarily. Like a naughty child at the 'all, you can eat' ice cream factory it will always want more no matter how much it gets, even if more of what you crave is, in the long run, detrimental to your well being. It is for this reason alone that giving a person the exact amount of money they have declared will bring peace is only useful as a temporary sticking plaster solution to their problems. Very soon reasons, why that amount was too conservative, begin to emerge.

Unhappiness, pain, and misery are human emotions created directly by the ego to manipulate the desired response. These painful feelings are generated by the 'thinking mind' when it doesn't get what it wants but also instead ironically also directly as the result of giving it precisely what it wants too, and such is the insanity!

Think of the soul/subconscious as silent but powerful and the ego as noisy but weak, because the ego has his hand in the air and is screaming for our attention we get mixed up about which part of us is soft and which part is powerful. It is natural to assume the element of our being that is jumping up and down and assuring us that it knows what to do is the best holder of the ray gun. This is wrong, wrong, wrong – we inadvertently give the keys to the asylum to the most dangerous inmate.

The ego insists it knows how to use the ray gun to give you what you want. Like a baby who has just had its lollypop taken from him, it will scream blue murder until you give it what it wants. But, your ego can achieve peace only for the tiniest fragment of time, typically immediately after you give it what it wants. For the briefest of moments, it affords you a small break from the insanity and stops relentlessly punishing and manipulating you. When the sedation begins to fade the ego reawakens as hungry as a grizzly bear stirring from a long hibernation. It demands more of what you gave it before but ten times stronger and will not accept anything but your capitulation, sending massive pain in the form of a hundred different negative emotions such as jealousy, low, and self-loathing until it gets what it desires. This is the exact reason why 95% of diets fail, trying to arm wrestle the egoic mind into submission with a technique incorrectly labeled as 'willpower' is like trying to move a mountain with a spoon.

Nobody has ever achieved anything with 'willpower' because it's an oxymoron there is no power involved in it at all! The ego cannot be strong-armed into submission by defiance; it has you outgunned on every level. Your ego has the power to cause you pain beyond your wildest nightmares, and it isn't afraid to use it. The only way you achieve anything of significance in life and beat the discontentment of the ego is by harnessing the divine power of the subconscious. At this level of being you are capable of endless joy, anything and everything is possible without the need for anything to make it possible. From mild contentment to perfect peace and everything in between your subconscious mind has the power to deliver it to you. This is what I call 'Manifesting Magic'; it is the other book of spells that you have rarely used. This book is in such pristine condition because you unwittingly asked the (insane) ego which book was best to use in order to get the life you want.

Until this point, I have carefully used the word subconscious when I would have preferred to say, soul. I do this deliberately because for me to expect you to accept the word soul (and all its connotations) I have to assume that you believe it exists in the first place. Virtually everyone agrees with the concept of a conscious and subconscious, I can comfortably bring these aspects of the human mind up nice and early in the book, but I wait until this point hoping to have whet your appetite before I appear to go 'all spiritual' on you!

For me, your soul and your subconscious are the same because what happens to you unconsciously and by that I mean without the interference of your ego or your thinking mind, happens with divine power. By divine I mean there is just nothing that is impossible if your soul or subconscious so desires it. Naturally, the first skeptical objection to this grand claim of miracles is challenging statements like 'if I am all-powerful, why aren't I rich already' and so on.

The more in-depth answer to that question you will discover as you journey through this book, but as a tempting morsel to keep you going; and of course to avoid 'question dodging' accusations flaring up so early in our relationship as author and reader I would ask you to consider that it is only your ego that believes you need money to be happy. Anything that has its solution in the future is pure speculation of your conscious mind, one of those specific requirements of how happiness should be packaged for your consumption. Your soul doesn't believe anything; it desires nothing, needs nothing and it automatically knows what will make you happy.

As a natural born cynic myself, I will try and answer your logical objections as we discover these secrets together. By this point I understand that your mind is probably acting like the Hydra beast of Greek mythology; for every question, I answer two new ones appear to take its place. This is the ego again attempting to reassert its authority, and we have been taught from an early age to listen to it.

From childhood we are told that to want too much is to be greedy, rich people are immoral and somehow tainted by their own success. Conversely to not have enough money, to be poor is also judged to be a failure. We project this confusing concept out to the masses through our movies, books, television news and tabloid newspapers. We love the underdog until they become successful and then we demand that they are brought down a peg or two.

Society wants us to have 'just enough' but not quite enough to be happy – this is what we have collectively agreed is 'normal' which for some reason when you write it down appears to be quite insanely ridiculous. Our parents also subscribed to this standpoint, as did their parents and all who went before them. It's the bizarre relay race of the ego forever passing its delusions onto the next generation. This is demonstrated by our parents in the vocalized desire for us to work hard and get a 'good job' to ensure our future happiness. What parents mean by a 'good job' is a safe and secure job that may even be boring but is continuous. Rarely do parents hope and dream that their children will follow their heart, throw caution to the wind and take risky, dangerous but exciting jobs.

There are many millions of people around the world in the most menial and insignificant of low paid, unskilled jobs that are content with their lot and truly happy within themselves, but no parent would wish or encourage this lifestyle for their child. Instead, their aspirations for their young are generated from the ego, and they dream that they will be the world's next doctors, scientists, accountants, managers, and directors. Hopefully, along the way they will meet the man or woman of their dreams, settle down with a mortgage (a word derived from the Latin phrase meaning until death) have kids and live happily ever after, only to repeat the process. A list of handed down expectations that compound the belief that happiness is a destination achievable through the attainment or attachment to external things. They want this for us because it's what they want for themselves and therefore assume it is also the best that could happen to us. This belief is an oasis in the desert to the thirsty man, nothing but a pure illusion.

This cycle has been running in the western world for many thousands of years but recently levels of general unhappiness and frustration have begun to accelerate and magnify exponentially as a result of the stabilizing prop of traditional religion is starting to fail simultaneously. The discontented folk could previously be dissuaded from challenging the status quo with assurances that God has a place in heaven reserved for them, but only if they comply with the rules and dare not question the scriptures further.

In order to achieve abundance, we have to consider the reverse of that position, as a result of this premise of social programming you will find that this book is not an instruction manual or a journey of discovery. If anything it's about the opposite of learning, an unlearning experience where we slowly strip away the false beliefs that you have been programmed and burdened with since birth.

When a fishing trawler gets trapped in a violent storm what brings the respite is the removal of something and not the addition of something. The removal of the storm and a return to zero is what dissipates the sensation of peril and danger. As such, happiness is peace and peace is the absence of everything else and so it's illogical to assume we can find what we are looking for by creating rules or by attaining material possessions. Abundance comes as the direct by-product of happiness and is not the destination we are navigating to.

The secrets revealed in this course will change your life forever, and your discovery of it at this point in your life is no co-incidence. As the famous quotation goes; 'when the student is ready, the teacher will arrive' and for that reason, despite your excitement you cannot force this information onto others who do not seek it, do not expect them to receive the message with the same sense of wonder and excitement that you did.

Most people spend their entire lives trapped within the illusions of the egoic mind. That is not so surprising when you consider that research shows us that of all the things you hear in a 24-hour period, 80 percent of them are negative. The average 18-year-old male has been told 146,000 times no or you can't do it. Now this causes us a problem because of something I call the law of subconscious attraction (or subattraction for short). Basically you have delivered to you what you subconsciously know to be true. If you simply know, and I do mean absolutely 'know' that you are an overweight individual then that reality will be created for you whether it's currently true or not. If at a subconscious level you fundamentally believe life is meant to be spent struggling to pay the bills and living hand to mouth (Perhaps just like your parents did) then guess what happens.

The egoic world in which we live would have you believe a whole heap of negative bullshit because misery loves nothing better than company. In short, eighty percent of the world is throwing a pity party and has extended you a big fat invitation. At the moment you are still on the guest list and what I am suggesting to you; is that if you change your beliefs not only can you leave the others to their depressing party but you can join the world's elite twenty percent who want for nothing and live the life of their dreams.

Now, concentrate because here comes the science part. I have been using the Law Of Attraction to manifest the life of my dreams for nearly a decade now. I have gone from flat broke to being a millionaire, from a broken marriage to being married to the woman of my dreams, from living in the gloom and cold of the United Kingdom to a villa by the sea on a sun-drenched Mediterranean island. However, up until a few weeks ago, I had no way to prove it to you other than hoping you find my own story inspiring enough.

The reason I believe there is now zero doubt over whether the Law of Attraction works or not is down to something in our brain called the Reticular Activating System (RAS). We are sensory animals, and at any one time we are being bombarded with over 14,000,000 bits of information. Even sitting in an empty room would overload our brain with data if we didn't have some way to filter out the important from the irrelevant. For example, does it matter what color the walls of the room are if the temperature has suddenly dropped below freezing?

Yes, our minds are incredibly sophisticated. We can sort through billions of bits of data at any given time. And for some reason, so we don't short circuit, we have to organize that data. The Reticular Activating System assists with that.

The Reticular Activating System (RAS) is a collection of nerves in your brainstem that filters out unnecessary information so the essential stuff makes it through.

The RAS is the explanation you learn a new word and then start hearing it everywhere. It's the reason that you can disregard a crowd full of talking people, however immediately snap to attention when somebody mentions your name or something that at least resembles it.

Your RAS takes what you concentrate on and develops a filter for it. It then sorts through the data and delivers only the parts that are essential to you. All of this happens without you noticing, naturally. The RAS programs itself to work in your favor without you actively doing anything. Pretty awesome, right?

Similarly, the RAS seeks data that validates your beliefs. It screens the world through the parameters you give it, and your beliefs form those parameters. If you think you are weak at giving speeches and presentations, you probably will be. If you feel you work efficiently, you probably do. The RAS helps you see what you would like to see and in doing this, influences your actions.

Many people suggest that you can train your RAS by taking your subconscious thoughts and marrying them to your conscious thoughts. They call it "establishing your intent." This essentially means that if you concentrate hard on your objectives, your RAS will uncover the individuals, data and opportunities that help you achieve them.

If you love positivity, for instance, you will become more aware of and look for positivity. Have you noticed that when you make a carefully thought out decision to buy a specific brand and type of car you start seeing those automobiles everywhere you go. I thought long and hard about buying a Rolex, I had always been of the opinion that they are a beautiful watch, but it's hard to justify spending so much on something you wear on your wrist. Then when I decided I was going to treat myself, I started to see people wearing Rolex's everywhere.

When you examine it like this, The Law of Attraction does not seem so mysterious. Focus on the negative things, and you will invite pessimism and problems into your life. Concentrate on the great, and they will come to you because your brain is seeking them out. It's not magic; it's your Reticular Activating System affecting the world you observe around you.

Articles and scrappy YouTube videos suggest many ways to teach your RAS to get what you want, but I find this method to be the most practical:

First, think about the objective or circumstance you wish to influence.
Now think about the experience or result you want to reach in regards to that goal/situation.

Create a mental motion picture of how you envision that goal/situation preferably turning out in the future. Notice the noises, dialogues, aesthetic and particulars of that psychological movie. Replay it frequently in your head. Of course, in reality, these things aren't as easy as they sound, but I do think that our Reticular Activating System (RAS) can be instructed. It's about visualizing what we want, and after that allowing our unconscious and conscious collaborate to make it happen.

The idea is: If I can hear my own name in a crowd of thousands, can I also tune my brain to focus and attract the essential things that matter to me? I'm reasonably sure I can. This is why I keep my 421 Journal with me anywhere I go, and reread it frequently. I have to continually refocus and remind my mind what matters and what does not. Don't worry I will tell you all about the pure power of the 421 later in the book.

My mission in life is to understand it, to take it apart, catalog the components and put it back together again. Then to take what I have learned to help other people understand. I have always had this fascination with how stuff works. I used to horrify my family when I was a child, they would buy me an expensive toy as a gift and the first thing I would do is take it apart until it was a thousand pieces on the living room carpet. I would even do this when my parents were not around and with their stuff, like my Dad's record player or my mum's hairdryer. You have heard the expression that curiosity killed the cat, right? In my case that is very nearly true, I can remember getting several serious electric shocks as a result of disassembling high voltage equipment to understand how it worked.

Back when I was a teenager, one day I decided to dismantle the telephone. I spent a few hours dissecting this noisy beast on my operating table before deciding to put it back together before my mother came home and went crazy. As was often the case, it went back together easy enough but I was left with three or four screws and bits that I could not remember where they were supposed to go. As a result, when I tried the telephone it would not work. Instead of a dialing tone, there was silence. I took the device apart again and tried once more to rebuild the family phone. No luck, still as dead as a dodo. My mother would be home any minute, I was in serious trouble unless I could fix the telephone in the next few minutes. I remembered my Grandad had a little trick for testing if a 9-volt battery still had power inside it. I am certainly not recommending this but he would stick his tongue on the elements and declare that it was good or bad. In my moment I made a couple baseless assumptions:

1. That technique even worked
2. That the voltage of a UK telephone line was 12 volts

So, with absolutely no knowledge, skill or common sense I decided to test the main cable into the phone to see if it was live. I touched my tongue to the wire expect a small but not painful shock to confirm the power was flowing. The biggest mistake I made was assuming the voltage was 12 volts, it wasn't, it was 50 volts. It sent me flying backward into my mum's favorite coffee table and gave me a headache that lasted for about 3 days.

So it doesn't surprise me that today I take human beings apart (not literally) and try to understand what makes them tick. I notice from examining myself that there are some areas of my life where I am supremely confident and as a result success just seems to flow unrestricted. Yet, the same cannot be said for all areas of my life and in some things, I am paralyzed by fear and self-doubt and I see very poor performance in these areas. What fascinates me about this is the person we are talking about is the same person. What I wanted to know is why I can be unstoppable at one thing and ineffective and lame at another. The conclusion I came down to is all about belief. You are what you believe yourself to be.

This is very exciting because it means if you get your thinking correctly aligned you are practically limitless. Of course, because everything life is balanced and you can't have good without bad or sweet without sour. If your inner perception is wrong then you can easily end up living a life somewhere between mediocre and miserable. I have always been very stubborn and resistant to rules. Pretty much everything I have achieved in my life has been against a very vocal chorus telling me that what I want is impossible and I am silly for even trying.

My father, the second youngest of eight children had a tough working-class upbringing in an overcrowded, under-resourced household in the North East of England. His father was a strict disciplinarian and his belt often dealt with any misbehavior swiftly and severely.

As soon as my father got the opportunity he set about creating a life free of that sense of fear and scarcity. He started his own business, and to ensure its success for over forty years he toiled at it from 5 o'clock in the morning until late evening, seven days a week. His goal was to ensure that his children would never experience the harshness of life that he endured growing up. Solid as a rock, he is a man who is firmly rooted in the real world, a student and graduate of the school of hard knocks. A solid believer that nothing in life is for free and everything is achieved through hard work and hard work alone.

Because of his tough background and his real-world evidence that work is a serious business when as a teenager I told him I wanted to be a radio presenter he told me I was ridiculous and I should stop messing around with something that will never happen and get a proper job. That sounds harsh I know but at the time it was like water off a duck's back. It didn't make the slightest dent in my confidence because I didn't just want to be on the radio I knew with every fiber of my being that I would be. At age 17 I became the youngest morning show host in the United Kingdom. After many years moving to bigger and bigger radio stations I started to lose interest in what I was doing. I once again went back to my father and told him that now I was going to run radio stations for a living. Again he told me to stop dreaming and get real. He said 'you are a DJ not a businessman, stick to what you know and don't risk the job you have'. Again I heard nothing and quickly became the programme director of two multimillion pound, heritage radio stations. When I later told my dad that I was giving up the radio to become an author and success coach you can imagine how insane he thought I was.

When it comes to career, business and following my passion I am unstoppable. I firmly believe that if I wanted to become an astronaut or a brain surgeon I could do it. My self-belief is so strong that nothing anyone could say would break my spirit or stop me achieving my goals. And yet, that belief structure does not run through my entire life. Recently at a crazy training event in Bangkok Thailand, several times a day they would stop the presentation to play dance music. This was done every time the speaker noticed that energy levels in the room were going down. The music would be called for and everyone told to stand up and dance. Now you know how I feel about dancing in public so my heart is already on the floor by this point. But it gets worst, they would also pull random people up onto the stage and have them dance for the audience. It's like someone has been recording my nightmares and tried really hard to make them solid. So whenever that bloody music started up I would leave the room.

Here's the strange thing, before I because a radio presenter I wasn't afraid to be one and before I was an author I had no doubt that I would change lives with what I do. So why can I not apply the same mindset to the simple act of dancing? Why are you awesome at some things and not at others? The answer is all around you right now! We are hugely affected by our environment and the people in it. If you want to know who you are, look at the five people who you spend the most time with. We all tend to become an average of the people we share our lives with. This is why I tell people who come to my Quit Drinking Bootcamp that some people you currently call 'friend' will have to leave your life. Drinkers like the company of other drinkers because it gives them social proof that validates their behavior. However, safety in number (however erroneous) is never a good enough reason for a relationship. The people around you should be lifting you up and pushing you forward but for the most part this is not the case.

Does this mean the people around you don't love you? Of course not, if anything they perhaps love you too much. Let me explain that statement; your parents, partner, family and close friends love you and care about you. They want to keep you safe from harm and it is for this reason they encourage you to stay in your comfort zone. Our comfort zone is a wonderfully warm, cozy and safe place but nothing ever grows there. Your purpose, passion and pretty much everything worth having are just outside the edge of your comfort zone. Your loved ones don't want you to go out there because there is a great deal of risk. You could get hurt or worse still end up feeling disappointed. So, they encourage you to stay safe and protected even though ultimately it will lead to a mediocre life and a profound sense of unfulfillment.

The most empowering thing your family can do for you is to give you TOUGH LOVE. To push you out of your comfort zone because they know that it will eventually lead to a better life. This is super difficult to do and I know first hand being the dad to two grown-up children. My biggest challenge as a father is resisting the urge to fix everything. As you know I live in Cyprus these days but my daughter lives in the UK and my son lives in San Francisco. Anytime they call feeling down, upset or with a big problem to solve it takes all my willpower to not book a flight immediately and go fix their lives for them. This will make them happy in the short term but it will only lead to long-term misery. I believe allowing someone you love to suffer (short-term) pain because you can see the bigger picture is one of the most challenging actions you will ever undertake.

My father did not tell me I could not be a radio presenter because he doesn't love me and doesn't want me to achieve my dreams. Quite the opposite is true, he loves me so much that he doesn't want me to follow a path that he envisions will only lead to failure, pain, and disappointment. When I was earning big money as the director of UK radio stations and I told my father that I was giving it up to become an author and motivational speaker every alarm bell in his head went off and he tried to discourage me to protect me, but never to hold me back. The same is true in your life and in the life of every human being alive. There are people who love you so very much that they want to keep you safe forever.

Sadly, 'forever' does not exist in any form in our world. Everything living, everything nature placed here and everything we build will eventually crumble and fall. Nothing is saved; death and destruction are like the outward breath of God. He breathes in and life is created, trees grow and buildings emerge. He breathes out and people die, trees burn to the ground and buildings collapse.

Sadam Hussain spent a lifetime building as many statues in his image as possible, he commissioned hundreds of portraits to be painted and even officially named Iraq's main airport Sadam Hussain International Airport. He did all this in a vain attempt to live on after his death – he failed. Virtually all the statues were pulled down and the airport was renamed.
If you are pinning your happiness and success in life on achieving permanency then you are destined to fail. At the end of your days when you lay in your deathbed considering your vast property portfolio and the millions of dollars in the bank, you can be sure that you would happily trade it all for just one more week alive.

More subtly than that we all also get attached to the idea of permanency when we give ourselves labels. Do you not think at some point when Adolf Hitler was growing up his mother sat him on her knee and said 'Adolf you are such a good little boy'. Was she wrong, or perhaps she was right but only at that moment?

All too often we take these labels and decide that they are a permanent description of who we are.

- I am a good person (how do you know you always will be?)
- I am a fast sprinter (will that always be the case)
- I have high standards; I will never stay in a hotel with less than

a 5 star rating (Never?)

When I coach people one to one they normally approach me with a label that they have decided is permanent. They come up to me and say 'I am a terrible public speaker, I always make a fool of myself' or 'I have terribly bad luck, nothing ever goes right for me'.

If you believe there is anything about your life that is permanent then I want you to spend some time thinking about how that could possibly be true in a world where it's impossible. I apply this just as much to the good stuff as the things we call 'bad'. I would call myself a 'good parent'; I love my children deeply and without question. However, I am willing to admit that at times I have made mistakes, given bad advice, shouted when I should have hugged and generally been a 'bad' parent. Especially during the challenging teenage years where my kids were striving to break free and be individuals. So which am I? 'A bad parent' or 'a good parent'? In reality, no label serves any useful purpose beyond the moment it is expressed in.

Good times will end and life will blindside you with events that spoil the fun. In the dark times, the storm will come to an end and bright sunshine will once again fill your life. This is the ebb and flow of the universe – divinity will breathe in and divinity will breathe out.

I know my family only wanted to keep me safe, but if I had listened to my father back then I would not be here today. I love my life, everything about it and I feel like the luckiest man alive. Is that not the outcome my parents always dreamed about for me? Sure, but often the people who love you the most are not the ones who know what's best for you in the long run. This is a powerful fact that I have to keep reminding myself about every day as a father of two unique children out there on their own mission in life.

The truth is everything that appears in your life is a reflection of what is inside you. Your beliefs dictate how much love, money, sex, success and well, just about everything you have in your life today. If there is an area on that wheel of life you created earlier in the book that needs work, then all you have to do is change your beliefs and hey presto. If you are responding to that last statement with any of the following:

Easier said than done
You don't know how much bad stuff has happened to me Craig
I have tried to fix it and I just can't
The problem is not me it's other people

I wish I was there to slap you roundly about the chops. Every single one of those excuses is 100% pure grade horseshit. To prove it, I want to tell you about my friend Nick.

Nick is a motivational speaker like me, but he is much more popular. He travels around the world with his team, he gets to visits the most wonderful places on this planet, traveling in style and staying in super comfortable hotels. He never goes to an office, never has to worry about the morning commute to work and where ever he goes people fall in love with him. If you have any sensation of envy about my friend let me give you some context to reframe that state you have there:

Nick Vujicic was born without any arms or legs. The closest thing he has to a useable extremity is what should have been his left leg. Looking nothing like a human foot, it is a small protrusion that he affectionately refers to as his chicken drumstick. He uses the limited motion of this appendage to control his electric wheelchair.

Can you imagine what childhood was like for this guy? He grew up always feeling different, always feeling left out. Watching his friends run, jump and play soccer. Always the spectator and never the protagonist. Sure he has had his moments of despair and openly admits that he has been to some dark places, but he chooses to do the opposite of what you would expect. Rather than wallow in his misfortune, he chooses to embrace the life he has been given. Despite all the odds, he is an exceptionally talented and popular motivational speaker. He tours the world speaking to schoolchildren about positive thinking and self-esteem.

If you have never heard of this guy, I encourage you to get on YouTube and watch some of his videos, if he doesn't move you to tears within a few minutes I insist you get checked for a working heart as soon as possible.

When Nick goes to speak to a group of children they normally watch in stunned silence as he is helped onto a table at the front of the assembly hall. The severely disabled and yet smiling man in front of them mesmerizes the ordinarily raucous group of youngsters. Such is the stillness in the room that you could hear a pin drop. Nick breaks this profound silence by challenging them to a game of soccer, and a nervous laugh fills the room. Nick Vujicic is so full of positive, loving energy that it causes the whole room to radiate with the most incredible and tangible peace.

By the end of the talk, the dozens of girls who had previously cried themselves to sleep thinking about the words of a bully are now crying in joy and love for the man who found happiness against all odds. Love pours out of every cell in this guy's little body as he sits there propped up on a table and dares to ask the kids if they think he is beautiful. Without a flicker of hesitation or doubt the whole room agrees that he is an amazing and stunningly beautiful person. There is a very real mass awakening as children realize the true gift of their own life. The child who hates her freckles suddenly realizes just how perfect she is. The boy who is bullied for being overweight suddenly understands his true worth. Every child sees their potential.

But surely when it comes to sex and women Nick has a valid excuse, right? No, a few years ago Nick Vujicic married his sweetheart, and let me tell you, she is stunningly beautiful. They now have an amazing, healthy son and if you see pictures of Nick and his wife you will see two of the happiest people you ever saw. The beautiful woman at his side is a reflection of the man inside the body. Nick Vujicic is full of love, he is aware of his limitations, but he believes that he is a valuable human being with the ability to enhance the lives of all those around him. But the single most important aspect of Nick's success is he is not a victim. Of course, he had the choice to become a victim, many times. But he chose to see the opportunities rather than the obstacles.

If you think Nick is a one-off and you still believe you have a valid excuse to defend not having the wealth, abundance, happiness and amazing life that you desire then I will remind you of the story of W. Mitchell:

In 1971, June 19th, he was 28 years old. He didn't have a care in the world. He was a very good-looking guy. He was driving down the freeway in America on his motorbike and not a care in the world. Something caught his attention to the left in a field, and he looked to see what it was. When he turned back to concentrate on the road, he realized he was traveling at 80 miles an hour towards the back of a truck. He was only 5 ft. away from the truck.

The only thing he could do to save his life was to slam the bike onto the floor so he would slide under the truck. As he slid under the truck, the fuel cap came off the motorbike and covered him in gasoline. The sparks from the motorcycle ignited the fuel. He was ablaze. Sixty-five percent of his body had third-degree burns. His face was nearly burnt off. His fingers were stumps. He was unrecognizable. People would visit him in the emergency ward of the hospital and pass out when they saw him. He was that bad.

He was in a coma for two weeks and when he came round would you have blamed him if he said, I can't go on; life is just not worth living? W. Mitchell chose a different path. He realized after a time that he didn't have to accept society's notion that to be happy a person must be healthy and good looking. Mitchell came to see it, as he put it I'm in charge of my spaceship, my own ups, and downs. I can choose to see this as either a setback or a new beginning.

Instead of being overcome by his apparent problems and the pain of the therapy he'd have to go through, Mitchell decided to turn those problems into challenges. He joined two friends, and he founded a new wood-burning stove company. A few short years later he helped build Vermont Castings into a multimillion-dollar company. He was a millionaire. If you think that's the happy ending of the story, think again.

In 1975, November, disaster struck again. W. Mitchell was sitting on the runway in his private jet with three friends in the back. He'd forgotten to check the wings for ice and as you probably know ice can cause disaster for planes. As he attempted to take off the plane crashed. His three passengers got out without a mark on them. W. Mitchell was paralyzed from the neck down. Mitchell chose to survive, and those negative people went up to him and said, somebody must really hate you up there, how are you going to continue? He said, before all this happened there were 10,000 things I could do. Now there are only 9,000. I could spend my life dwelling on the 1,000 that I lost, or I could choose to focus on the 9,000 that are left, and that's what he did.

In 1982 he married his sweetheart, and in 1984 he ran for Congress. He went door-to-door campaigning, and he used the catchphrase, vote for me and I won't be just another pretty face. Mitchell says that he had two big bumps in his life and he chose not to use them as excuses to quit. To become a success, to become wealthy, concentrate on the positive.

Nick Vujicic and W. Mitchell focused on what they have and not what they don't have. Anytime you are moving toward something good you are powerful and every time you are running away from something bad you are in a position of weakness. That sounds like something easy to do but I understand it's hard to think about where you want to get to when there is a lion chasing you right? Sadly 80% of the population spend their entire life running away from what they don't want. Debt chases people like a hungry lion and while most people want to be wealthy they can never change their state enough to stop running.

Your beliefs and state are entirely internal and they dictate who you are as a person and what you achieve in this life. This is fantastic news because it means that you don't need anyone else to get the life you want, you don't need to save up to buy it and you couldn't even if you wanted to. This is a level playing field and it doesn't matter where you come from, what physical ability you have, your gender, race or anything else that makes you different to the next guy. If Nick can do it, if Mitchell can do and Bethany can do it - there is absolutely no reason why you can't do it.

Are you ready to find out how?

Great, the answer is really simple. Be like JJ.

Cyprus has a huge animal abuse problem, the state does virtually nothing to tackle it and the while the mindset of the people is improving there are still many people who see animals as worthless and disposable. This is tough if you are an animal lover like me because it means you can't help but see a lot of suffering, abandonment, and misery. I am afraid when it comes to animals I can't walk away if I can help I will help. This is why we have far too many pets in our house. We have rescued three dogs and four cats from pretty miserable conditions.

This is JJ, he couldn't walk when we found him as a kitten. He had been thrown out of a car window by the garbage bins outs.

He would drag his back legs around after him. Our vet told us that he believed it was a neurological problem and he would never be able to walk properly. Today, out of all the cats JJ not only walks just fine, but he is also the best hunter, the fastest runner, and most bad attitude 'take no shit from nobody' cat. You see, when JJ looks in the mirror he doesn't see a little cat, he sees a mighty lion. This is a mindset that cats are awesome at, do a quick search on Google and you will hundreds of videos of cats kicking the asses of dogs ten times their size. There is one video that has gone viral many times of a cat hitting an aligator in an argument over some meat on the edge of the river. I am telling you here and now if there was ever a civil war in our house and cats took on the dogs, the cats would win easily - despite being a fraction of the size. Dogs think as dogs and cats think like lions, that's the secret.

What JJ teaches us all is if you want something then live it, breathe it and embody it. If you want a promotion at work act like you are already doing the job. If you want an amazing relationship then act like you are in one. Be the best girlfriend, boyfriend, wife or husband that you can imagine. You may resist that statement and many before you on the QUIT DRINKING BOOTCAMP event has raised a hand at this point and said but my husband doesn't appreciate me, so why bother? Hey, this is never about the other person - everything you ever wanted already exists inside you. Don't you see that JJ does not think like a lion for my benefit or for the approval of the other cats, he could not care less what anyone else thinks. JJ is a lion because he IS A LION. You have to be the change you want to see in the world. You should trust me on this when you raise your standards one of either two things will happen. The people around you will follow or they will leave. If your husband or wife can't appreciate you at your best then there will be someone out there desperate to take their place. You are freaking awesome and you deserve the best right?

What stops people being a little bit more JJ? Just one four letter word is the source of all our challenges - fear and that's what we are going to obliterate next.

SECTION FOUR – REFRAMING FEAR

THE DRIVERS AND PASSENGERS OF LIFE

When I was a younger man, the world looked a very different place. I thought that success was largely down to a mix of talent and luck — two things that you could not possibly ever control. I didn't realize it at the time, but I had entirely defaulted to the standard victim thinking that the majority of people adopt.

They say that youth is wasted on the young and I believe that's completely right. Over the years I have watched how people respond to the challenges and obstacles in life. I have even had the privilege of being a father and observing how two new people get to grips with the world and struggle to find their place in it. What I have concluded is that a lot of people never manage to bust out of victim mode. So many people spend an entire lifetime throwing a pity party of massive proportions, and everyone is invited!

Life is not like a box of chocolates at all! I believe that life is like a plane journey. Most of the people taking the trip are passengers, very few people decide to be the driver. Now, these passengers are a diverse bunch. Some of them know where the train is going and don't mind one bit. Some of them know where the train is headed and are mighty annoyed at the driver because of it. Others haven't got the first clue where they are going or how long it will take to get there. However, despite their varied states of mind, they all share one common position. None of them are completely content and at peace with the journey.

Even the relatively happy passengers have no say in where they are going, how fast the train will travel or how comfortable the journey will be. Only the driver has that privilege. The driver of the train gets the very best seat, right up front with the most amazing views. He gets to decide where the train is going, how quick it will get there, and he even takes control of environmental controls so that he can set the temperature and humidity to suit himself entirely.

The path of least resistance is to buy a ticket and get on the train. The more difficult road is to apply for the position of a train driver, undertake many months of intensive training, spend the first few weeks of the job way out of your comfort zone as you become responsible for the lives and safety of several hundred people every time, you take that train out of the station. Only after you have invested time, effort and money in your decision do you get to reap the rewards. This is a perfect analogy for life.

Everything of value lies just outside our comfort zone.

It's true that I have had many people argue with that statement. Have you ever noticed that some people are always looking for ways to be offended? Especially on social media. I guarantee you that if I post that very same statement on Facebook today, by tomorrow, I will have dozens of very offended people commenting. They will state that family and friends are inside the zone and they are perhaps the most valuable aspect of life. But maybe they won't phrase it as politely as that.

They are as right as they are wrong!

It is true that your family, partner, and friends are gifts that no money or amount or hard work could ever replicate. However, there is a vast difference between having children and being a father. There are a million miles between spending time with other people and being their friend. If you have little ones of your own, you will no doubt agree with me that you discovered with a shock that the role of being mother or father to those kids is a long walk from the outer edges of your comfort zone.

So, I will repeat it. Everything of value lies just outside of our comfort zones. That is precisely why most people never get the life that they want. That is why tens of millions of people endorse the garbage they churn out on television every night, and that is why the majority of people will work a job they don't like, for a boss who doesn't appreciate them to stay in a relationship that doesn't fulfill them. But enough of this bleak outlook, this book is not for those people. This book is for the driver of the train, or at the very least the person who aspires to be the driver of the train.

Over the years I have listened to a lot of motivational speakers, and I do not doubt that you will see little inflections of my favorites in my style of writing here and there. Some of the in-spirational authors who have inspired and motivated me over the year include Tony Robbins, Brian Tracy, Alan Watts, Eckhart Tolle, and Zig Ziglar. These men write the sort of wisdom that my father would instantly dismiss as snake oil or worse. I was brought up by working-class parents from a background of hardship and hard knocks. My mom and dad would even keep a coffee jar on top of the TV to pop coins in, to save up for the electric bill. But eventually, my father shook off his background and escaped poverty by bloody hard work and persistence. His journey out of the abyss would lead him to look at anything that suggested a more easy way of doing things and declare it a scam or downright lies.

When I would quote motivational speakers such as Zig Ziglar, who made grand statements such as 'you can have anything you want in life' and 'you were born to win.' My father couldn't help but discard it all as new age nonsense. I can understand this skepticism because most people experience life sitting on the sidelines watching other people get lucky and get more than their fair share. Individuals in the 80% (the term that I use to describe the passengers on the train) are told over and over again that life is hard, life is not fair, and the system is stacked against them. They are taught this mantra by the people who they love and trust the most, their family. Despite how it first appears, this message is not being passed down the line to cause misery. Instead, my father told me all these motivational speakers I was listening to were peddling snake oil because he wanted to protect me. God forbid we get our hopes up and dare to dream that life can be deeply fulfilling, more than fair and profoundly rewarding.

As I sit here at my desk at the age of 44, I can tell you that is precisely what life is. My life is breathtakingly beautiful. This year I married the woman of my dreams, I live on a Greek island in the sun, my house is 3km from the beach, I have more money than I know what to do with and I don't ever go to work. Good for you Craig, and thanks for rubbing my nose in it. Is what I hope you are not thinking! I am not telling you that to boast because I firmly believe when you get an Unleashed mindset the very same or much better is possible for you too.

I don't know if you have noticed this, but the universe is always in perfect balance. As much as we fight against it, there can never be anything other than harmony. Birth is counterbalanced precisely by death; nobody has ever got away with it. No matter how much you pray, beg or plead, ain't nobody getting out of this alive. There is as much love as there is hate, although the media can skew our opinion on this.

The black and white wheel of yin and yang is always spinning, success balancing failure and love equaling out hate. I believe that virtually all of our misery comes from the refusal to accept the way of things. Our utter refusal to recognize that the wheel keeps turning, nothing is permanent. This viewpoint is then combined with our instance that things and events that appear to be opposite are separate from each other. We want success, but we do not want failure, we assume that because both outcomes are at polar ends of the spectrum that they are two different things. Most self-made individuals understand that success and failure are the same things. You can't have success without failure. To fall short of your goal and suffer is merely a waypoint on the route to your destination.

The passengers on the train don't want failure so much that they are willing to forego success to avoid it. They incorrectly assume that if taking action put you at risk of failure then doing nothing will prevent that outcome. However, the problem with this sort of thinking is it still incorrectly assumes that you can split success and failure in two. If this were possible, then the universe would be out of balance as a result. By doing nothing, you may avoid the risks and pitfalls of opportunity, and you are free to chalk that one up as a success if you want. But you will still arrive at failure regardless.

We get very hung up on giving labels to things. We lose $50 in the street and declare how terrible it is and yet if we find $50 we skip to work with a spring in our step, announcing to all who will listen that we are one lucky son of a gun. The person who lost the money labels the event as bad, and the lucky individual who finds the money labels it as good. How the same 'thing' be both good and bad at the same time? The answer from our point of view is, it can't. However, we are not viewing reality, only our narrow band of reality. The universe does not see good and bad as individual states. They are both connected to the same wheel of yin and yang.

Have you noticed that many of the world's wealthiest, most successful people in business have a trail of destruction in their wake? It is not uncommon for highly capable entrepreneurs to have multiple bankruptcies and company liquidations in their past. I am sure at the time those experiences were harrowing and were therefore labeled as terrible times for the individual.

However, when you look at the big picture, they turned out not to be 'bad' but lessons, valuable lessons.

When I was 35 years old, I got fired for the first time in my life, and it hit me like a sledgehammer. I was a very highly paid radio personality in the United Kingdom, but those types of job were like rocking horse poo, tough to find. I was being paid handsomely, but I was broke. My outgoings were way beyond what was coming it. So, when I lost my job and knew that it was going to be close to impossible to replicate the opportunity, I went into a blind panic. I felt like my whole world was collapsing around me. I had visions of my family and I being rendered homeless. I saw my children in dirty clothes, scraping by in abject misery. Without this traumatic event and the powerful lessons I learned from it I would not be where I am now. I let me tell you, I love where I am now.

No matter which path you choose, whether you take the risk and excitement of being the driver or opt for the apparent safety and security of just being a passenger. You are going to experience failure - there is no avoiding it. The only decision you have to make is, do you want your successes to mean something? You can be successful at preventing risk, or you can be successful at following your passion and living the life of your dreams.

Choose one!

FEAR TECHNOLOGY

Human behavior appears to be involved and multilayered, but in reality, it comes down to two simple elements. All human motivation is essentially a binary process, meaning that we are moved to either do something or avoid doing something by a single switch in our head being in one position or the other. All decisions, actions, and deeds are made as a result of us either avoiding fear or pursuing pleasure, and that is pretty much it. The reason for everything we do comes down to this simple premise.

We can spend hours debating the issue (as I have done many times before) but trust me on this one, even the generous actions of a parent for their child are still motivated by the emotions of fear and pleasure.

In the case of self-esteem and confidence, the fear that prevents us from performing as we could is 99.9% misplaced. Of course, sometimes the anxiety we feel most definitely has a place and I am not suggesting you ignore that little voice in your head that suggests you can't safely jump from one tall building to another. The fear you feel just before you do your first parachute jump is a process of the human mind operating precisely as it should. Making you feel afraid in these moments is a form of self-preservation. It is the brain's way of saying, 'hey if you continue doing what you are doing, there is an excellent chance you will die, and you will most likely take me along with you!'

But the fear that suggests that you are not attractive enough to talk to the hot girl is a misfire of this process. The gut-twisting anxiety you experience as you step up to make a presentation to the whole office is this life-saving feature of the human mind misunderstanding the situation and trying to force you to exit an environment it has incorrectly judged to be dangerous.

Confidence, or rather the lack of it, is a simple throwback to our earlier times as hunter-gatherers. Putting it another way, we are witnessing and experiencing the time lag of evolution trying to catch up with and adapt to what modern life involves. The life of a human being in the western world today has changed so dramatically over the last few hundred years that it is almost incomparable to what our forefathers had to endure. Today we get upset and feel like we have had a bad day if we can't find a parking space in the lot or spill our latte on our favorite t-shirt.

Compared to the life-threatening events that happened on a daily basis to the generations that went before us, our problems are embarrassingly trivial. As relatively recently as the 1800s, the average life expectancy of a human male living in the United Kingdom was 39 years. With disease, unsafe working conditions and vigilantly justice commonplace, someone at my tender age of 44 would be considered an old man. Perhaps my children have been correct all along when they insist I am incapable of appreciating their musical taste because I am so frail.

Bearing in mind that evolution is a painfully slow process that takes hundreds of thousands of years to make even the smallest adaptations to the design of our species, you can see why it is struggling to keep up with our rapidly changing modern lifestyles. While Apple may bring out a new model of its products every year, Mother Nature does not!

Back when we were at constant risk of being attacked by not only wild animals but also our fellow uncivilized man, the human mind developed systems to try and keep us alive despite the inherent danger around us. Perhaps the most famous of these is what we call the 'flight or fight' response.

When our fight or flight response is activated, sequences of nerve cells fire and potent chemicals like adrenaline, noradrenaline, and cortisol are released into our bloodstream. If you want to see how dramatic these chemicals are, get food poisoning and watch what happens. I can tell you from recent experience that your body uses these neurochemicals to make you dance like you are nothing more than a puppet on a string. When the body detects you have ingested something dangerous, like rotten food or too much alcohol, it needs to force you to evacuate the offending material, and it doesn't want to waste time debating this with you. Vast amounts of chemicals are released by the central nervous system that makes you feel incredibly ill, almost to the point where you feel like you are going to die. The next thing you know you are holding onto the toilet bowl as your life depended on it, screaming projectile vomit into the water. As a reward for doing as you were told, the body now releases mind-bending amounts of dopamine, which has the effect of making you feel instantly better—almost high. I don't advise you to experience food poisoning to verify this for yourself, just trust me.

My apologies, a rather unpleasant tangent sidetracked me there for a moment, though it was a good example. Now, getting back to how the mind instigates the flight or fight response. These patterns of neuro reactions and chemical releases force our body to undergo a series of very dramatic changes. Our respiratory rate increases. Blood is shunted away from our digestive tract and directed into our muscles and limbs, which require extra energy and fuel for running, fighting or maybe even both.

- Our pupils dilate
- Our awareness intensifies
- Our sight sharpens
- Our impulses quicken
- Our perception of pain diminishes.

- Our immune system mobilizes.
- We become prepared physically and psychologically for fight or flight.
- We scan and search our environment, looking for the enemy or threat.

When our fight or flight system is activated, we tend to perceive everything in our environment as a possible threat to our survival. By its very nature, the fight or flight system bypasses our rational mind—where our better thought out beliefs exist, and instead, it moves us into "attack" mode. This state of alertness causes us to perceive almost everything in our world as a possible threat to our survival. As such, we tend to see everyone and everything as a potential enemy. Like airport security during a terrorist threat, we are on the lookout for every possible danger.

We may overreact to the slightest comment. Our fear is exaggerated. Our thinking is distorted. We see everything through the filter of possible danger. We narrow our focus to those things that can harm us. Fear becomes the lens through which we see the world.

Our fight or flight response is designed to protect us from the proverbial saber tooth tigers that once lurked in the woods and fields around us, threatening our physical survival. On those occasions when our actual physical survival is threatened, there is no more significant response to have on our side. When activated, the fight or flight response causes a surge of adrenaline and other stress hormones to pump through our body. This surge is the inexplicable force responsible for mothers lifting cars off their trapped children, and for firefighters heroically running into blazing buildings to save endangered victims. The rush of adrenaline infuses us with heroism and courage at times when we are called upon to protect and defend the lives and values we cherish.

While this protective routine still has a valid place in our lives, it does not need to be activated nearly as frequently as it is, and certainly not in situations that lack true danger, such as making a PowerPoint presentation at work!

But I think that 'flight or fight' is an incorrect moniker for this automatic response to stress. There is a missing F in that much-quoted saying. The more common reaction in situations deemed to be high risk is not to fight or flee, but rather to freeze.

Fight, Flight or FREEZE

I am sure at times you have felt that 'deer in the headlights' sensation, where you know what is expected of you but somehow just can't bring yourself to move. There are no mistakes in nature and obviously removing your conscious ability to run, is a feature designed by evolution. If a giant brown bear enters your immediate environment and your subconscious programming decides that the best chance you have to remain alive is to play dead, then the last thing it wants is your pesky (and weak) conscious mind to have a say on the decision. So it locks you down, and despite how much you want to move, you find that it is virtually impossible.

When you freeze before making a speech or feel like your tongue has been paralyzed the very moment the beautiful woman starts to talk to you, this is merely the mind misreading the situation as dangerous and firing off one of your self-preservation routines. Of course, the big question is, how do you stop doing this?

The answer to this question and the beginning of a life full of abundance and success lies in the following pages. All I ask at this point is that you don't try to skip ahead and find the magic bullet. You will see no such thing; no one sentence can independently build your confidence. Success, as with everything else in life, is not about the final destination. It is all about the journey.

What I have discovered in life is that pretty much anything worth having is just slightly outside your comfort zone. Whether it's launching your own business, winning the league in your chosen sport, getting the career you have dreamed of or ending up with the man or woman who makes you feel like you just won the lottery every moment you are with them. None of these things are inside your comfort zone, they all require you to stretch and grow before you can reach them. As most people know, the walls of your comfort zone are made of a solid material called fear. To smash through these barriers, you have to stare fear straight in the eyes and charge ahead regardless.

At my QUIT DRINKING BOOTCAMP events I tell people that they need to make friends with fear. I show them how I recognize fear, not as a warning or an obstacle, but instead as an indicator of an opening window of opportunity. I have learned that when I am afraid to do something, the universe is telling me clearly and precisely what I have to do next. Fear is a powerful sign to me that an opportunity to learn, develop and grow has arrived. What most people see as an obstacle, I have taught myself to see as the most potent gift anyone can get, and I am going to give the same paradigm to you, starting today.

Please don't make the mistake of thinking that I am different to you or that I was born with a load of super brave DNA. That is not true. There were elements of life that terrified me, literally paralyzed me and rendered me frozen to the spot. I had to learn how to overcome these obstacles and at times it was not easy. Defeating fear has led me into some of the scariest situations in my life. However, what I have learned is that overcoming fear is a system, it can be written down as a recipe, just like the chocolate cake we talked about earlier in the book. I call this process 'Fear Technology' and it is a super exciting concept because it means that if you apply the blueprint to any aspect of fear in your life it will end in the same positive and rewarding outcome.

Don't worry I will tell you how to use Fear Technology shortly but first I want you to be aware that fear is present on a daily basis and in a myriad of ways. We are taught to be careful, to listen to fear and respond accordingly, and the vast majority of society obeys this unwritten law. The result is a safer, more boring and less fulfilling life. This is the world of the Average Joe and the Average Jane—safe and steady, but beige. What I am encouraging you to do is respond to fear in a highly counter-intuitive way. Instead of seeing fear as a warning, I want you to see it as an 'opportunity light' blinking on the dashboard of your life. Essentially, if you are afraid of it, then you must do it!

I can't begin to tell you how many people I meet who are full of regret, and it is virtually never about the things they have done in their life. Much more common are regrets about the things they didn't do. The last time I saw my aunty Angela, she had a coffee with my parents at their home in Darlington. I joined them all for a short while, and as I sat down, Angela was expressing her regret that she had never learned to drive. She had started to learn but got too afraid to ever put in for the test, and it just became one of those things we label shoulda, woulda, coulda. Two years previously, Angela had sadly been diagnosed with C.U.P. cancer (cancer of unknown primary origin). She was still her old lively self, but her prognosis was not great, all treatment had ultimately failed. The doctors estimated she had between six and nine months to live. Angela decided that before it became impossible, she was going to take and pass her driving test.

She never got the chance, as she died three weeks later. The moment she died, passing or failing that driving test became irrelevant; as did all the fear about taking the test in the first place. There are dozens of things that you want but don't have because fear is preventing you from going after them. One day in the future all that fear will be rendered pointless by the same event that Angela went through, the event that no one has ever managed to avoid. What I am saying is that your ego is trying to protect you from harm by encouraging you to avoid risk by using fear as a virtual 2x4 to hit you over the head with.

Your body is like an apartment shared between two tenants. The ego and the soul, or if you prefer, the conscious mind and the unconscious mind. These are the tenants of your body. The soul is eternal and divine, it is essentially a fragment of God, and it knows this for sure. It is also acutely aware that the apartment it is renting is temporary, and when the lease ends, it will just move to a new place and start over. However, the ego knows that when the contract ends, that's the end of the story, its game over. This creates a sensation of blind panic for the ego, which just flat refuses to accept the situation. It kicks and screams trying to prove that it can prevent the lease from ending. Hey perhaps if you fill the apartment with more and more stuff, and then never leave so they can't come in and dump your possessions, then perhaps the lease will continue evermore, right? The ego is so terrified of the end; it has been rendered insane by the constant thought of it.

Out of this insanity, we get all the self-limiting beliefs that hold us back.

- Save for a rainy day.
- What can go wrong, will go wrong.
- She's too hot for you; she will reject you.
- You are not ready for your driving test.
- You are not good enough for that promotion at work.

The ego uses the past as a reverse projector in an attempt to control the uncontrollable. Fear is liberally applied to all areas of your life with the hope that it will keep you safe, albeit entirely unfulfilled. You are alive but miserable, that's good enough. The ego doesn't particularly care how happy you are; its primary focus is trying in vain to avoid the inevitable final act, at whatever cost.

What I am about to ask you to do is acknowledge that one of your tenants is insane, and while you can't evict, you can decide to stop listening to his/her insane ramblings. From this point on, fear should be seen as the screams in the night of your troublesome tenant. All the predictions of doom, gloom, terror, and trauma are nothing more than a desperate illusion.

Start living in the knowledge that the only moment that exists is this one, right here and right now. The past and the future do not exist and they never will—this is it, and this is all there will ever be.

HOW TO DESTROY F.E.A.R USING FEAR TECHNOLOGY

Would you like to know how to overcome anything that you are afraid? Of course, you do, but I know you are not going to like it. There is no easy path on this one, and it's going to come down to how badly you want it. This is a good thing, if dealing with this was easy then firstly this book would not be, and equally, there would be no sensation of achievement and victory at doing something that the vast majority of people will never even consider.

Fear Technology works on the principle that what you push away always becomes stronger. It's a law of the universe in the same way that the electricity that comes through the wires in your house is never destroyed but rather converted into a different type of energy. Heat energy for the toaster and kinetic energy for the food mixer etc. When there is something you are afraid of, for example, spiders - and you push the fear away by running away screaming everytime you encounter an arachnid you are transferring energy to the very thing you want to move away from. The harder and more persistently you avoid this situation the deeper and more profound your fear will become. Can you see what's coming and why I said you will not like it?

Right back at the start of the book I asked you to draw your wheel of life where you gave each area of your life an rating from zero to ten. You will notice that in the romance and relationships section I gave myself a score of ten. I am head over heels in love with my wife. Daniela is my soulmate, my best friend and the most beautiful woman in the world. However, this is an area of my life that took me a very long time to get right and entirely because I was full of fear.

My parents in their wisdom decided that my brother and I should go to single-sex schools. I have never asked them for their reasons for sending Mark and me to all boys schools because I am still pissed about it. However, I am guessing that they figured we would concentrate on our school work more without the distraction of girls. Whatever their justification it left me in no doubt that I would never apply the same theory to my children. The biggest problem this created was at the age of sixteen, leaving school I didn't have the first clue how to talk to girls. I was terrified of them, and remember this is before the days of smartphones and Tinder. If you liked a girl, you had to walk up to her, often in front of all your friends and ask her for a date. This felt a bit like frying bacon naked, basically deliberately exposing your most sensitive parts to as much danger as possible. The crime is, I was a terrific looking guy in my youth, and now with a bit of age and wisdom I realize there were so many girls just dying for me to talk to them, but I was too afraid.

The result of this fear was that I approached girls very rarely and the first real relationship I got into pushed me right back into my comfort zone. It was safe and warm in that relationship, and I didn't have to risk exposing myself to rejection. The long-term relationship conveyor belt started up, and I started running. By nineteen I was living with someone, by twenty-three I was a father, and by twenty-six I was married. All this before I even knew who I was as a man. By the time I got into my thirties and started to understand myself a little better I knew I was in the wrong relationship. While it was comfortable it wasn't serving either of us anymore, we were no longer even sharing the same bed. We had become two strangers who happened to live in the same house.

It took a few years but we got divorced, and I found myself single for the first time in nearly two decades. Shit, the last time I dated there was no such thing as 'the internet'. Where does a thirty-seven-year-old divorced Dad go to find women?

The last time I was single the standard place to meet girls was a nightclub or bar. By this point in my life, it had been a good decade since I had even stepped foot inside a nightclub. I did try it, one Saturday I called up an old friend of mine and suggested we hit the town as we used to in the good old days. Boy, we were fired up as we queued to get into the club. I felt a huge rush of freedom and excitement. I allowed my mind to wander as we shuffled forward in the cold night air. I imagined hooking up with a stunning girl and taking her home at the end of the night for crazy, wild sex. When I got inside the venue, all my enthusiasm fell through the floor. I looked around at the girls busting their moves on the dance floor, and I suddenly felt like a pedophile. These girls looked only a little bit older than my daughter. I suddenly felt like the oldest man alive, like old father time had turned up to collect his daughter. At that moment I realized that everything I thought I knew about meeting women was wrong, out of date and useless to me.

A few days later I was at the Dentist, and while I was sitting waiting for my appointment, I picked up an old and well-worn copy of Cosmopolitan. An article on how more and more people are meeting in the aisles of supermarkets caught my eye. I decided that as soon as the anesthetic wore off and I didn't look and sound like the elephant man I was going to put some smart, cool clothes on and hit the supermarket, ready to meet the woman of my dreams.

For an hour I walked up and down those aisles with a loaf of bread and some soup in my basket. I saw perhaps half a dozen women I was attracted to, and I set out to approach all them. I would describe the outcome of that day a partial success. If by partial success you are willing to accept that I only had the guts to talk to one of them and all I managed to say was 'excuse me, do you know where the frozen food section is'? She pointed at an aisle at the opposite end, and I dutifully walked away, feeling like the biggest idiot on planet earth. The other five women may have been vaguely aware of a very pensive and stressed looking guy who kept walking up and down the same aisle as them, but the closest I got to sex that day was a brief flick through Bella magazine on the way to the checkout.

I was in trouble! I was a very successful, intelligent and reasonably attractive man with a lot to offer but I had no idea how to approach or talk to women. As I left that supermarket the words of my mother started to ring in my head. My parents have those old-fashioned values that state that despite how miserable you are, you stick at your marriage and honor the vows you made at the church. The day I told my mother that I was divorcing my wife she placed a caring hand on my cheek and said 'Oh Craig, what are you doing? You are too old for this nonsense, work at your marriage because you are not going to find someone else at this time of your life'. I mean, pretty much the worst thing she could have said to me at this powerfully tricky moment in my life – thanks a bunch Mom!

Remember when I said you don't find your purpose but you decide your purpose. At this moment I had a big decision to make, and like to do at the QUIT DRINKING BOOTCAMP events I started at the outcome. I knew what I wanted, a relationship with the most beautiful woman on planet earth. I am not just talking appearance because that stuff fades quickly. I wanted my soulmate, and I knew for sure she was out there. Now I had a target, and I could see it, I worked backward.

- Was I in the right environment to meet this woman?

Check!
- Are my values and beliefs congruent with the type of person I want to meet? Check!
- Am I behaving the way I want to be with this person? Check?
- Do I have the skills and capabilities to meet this amazing woman? Fail!

There was no way I could meet the woman of my dreams with such an essential spoke of the wheel broken like this. Despite how much I wanted that outcome a terrifying mountain of fear blocked the road to it. Even if fate threw me into the path of this amazing woman as it stood, I would only mess it up by stumbling, fluffing and panicking my way through an embarrassing retreat. Her lasting impression of me would be 'jeez, what's wrong with that loser.' I remembered that back when I decided to become a photographer, the first thing I did was book myself on a photography training course. This had to be the same logical step I would need to take in this case.

As my friend Grace tells me, I am not normal. So, I understand if you think this is a bit dramatic but I hired a coach to help me. A guy who had a fantastic reputation for building James Bond level self-confidence in guys. His name was Labi, and he was a very handsome and charismatic Latvian guy in his late twenties. I paid him a fair old chunk of money to spend the weekend with him in London. Over forty-eight hours he walked me up to the outer edge of my comfort zone and then he kicked me so hard out of it I thought I had died and landed in hell. On the first morning, I had barely said hello to him and taken a sip of my coffee when he pointed at a young woman walking down the street and said 'talk to her.' I laughed because I genuinely thought he was joking. He was not pointing at a woman he was looking at a catwalk supermodel. This girl must have been no more than nineteen years old, impossibly slim and beautiful — the sort of woman that they cast as the super hot character in a

Hollywood movie.

When I realized he was not joking and he was already a little angry that I had let her walk away my jaw dropped open in pure terror. Oh my good God what have I done, I thought! "No, no, no, you don't understand what I am here for," I said "I am a 37-year-old man, I know my limits, and I know what I want. There is no way a nineteen-year-old girl would be interested in me. Jeez, she would think her Dad was hitting on her'. He listened to me, but his expression didn't change once. Eventually, after a weirdly long and uncomfortable silence, he said 'That's a shame because I am not going to let you approach any woman less attractive than that for the next two days.'

"WTF! Surely this nut job can't be serious", I screamed inside. I started predicting total humiliation, destruction, and devastation. If you think there is a twist in the story coming and it turned out to be just fine, you are dead wrong. Over ten hours on that first day in London, Labi had me approach over thirty stunningly beautiful women. Every single one of them either ignored me, told me to fuck off or worse still just stared at me like I was some freak show. I fell into my hotel bed that night very much alone and entirely broken man. I felt like I was about three foot tall and least attractive man on planet earth.

I awoke the next day full of dread, not sure that I could take another day of pure hardcore rejection like that. But something had changed overnight; I think my subconscious had got to work on some of those fear routines in my brain. I noticed it the first supermodel he pointed to and told me to get her number. It wasn't that I thought I would actually get her number it's more that I no longer cared whether she rejected me or not. Being told no or worse was now such a common everyday experience to me I no longer gave it a second thought. So, I approached her with the mentality of 'I want you, BUT I don't need you.' Ten minutes later I was walking back to Labi an expression of pure shock on my face and phone number of a drop-dead beautiful twenty-one-year-old art student in my cell. At this moment it felt like someone had just proved to me that earth is flat. Nothing made sense anymore!

Labi looked at me and asked me a powerful question 'Now how difficult do you think it would be to approach a woman more your age.' I got it, the thing I had arrived being entirely terrified of now seemed as harmless and straightforward as brushing your teeth. You have probably heard statements like 'feal the fear and do it anyway' and 'you have the embrace your fears to conquer them'. However, Fear Technology states you have to go further than that -you have to expose yourself to infinitely more than you think you are capable of. You over train your fear muscles so that what you want to achieve becomes not only possible BUT effortless.

If any part of you thinks you can't replicate what I did, I will remind you that the world believe has the word 'lie' in it to highlight it to you. I felt that I was too old to be attractive to women younger than me. I believed that nobody would give me the time of day never mind their number. All limiting beliefs are lies - ALL OF THEM!

Exercise:

I want you to stop reading at this point and take a little life inventory. Grab a pen and paper and write down everything you can think of that you have ever wanted to achieve but have been prevented from doing so by fear. Perhaps you have always wanted to skydive, but can't quite bring yourself to sign up for a jump. Maybe there is a senior position opening at work, and you have told yourself that you are not quite ready and might try again in a few years. Perhaps you have been head over heels in love with Nicola on reception for years and never done anything about it?

On a blank piece of paper draw four columns, in the first column write your goal, in the second write down how fear is preventing you from achieving this goal, in the third column write down what will happen if you continue to let fear dominate this area of your life. In the final column, I want you to imagine how you would feel if you ignored the 'Danger, Do Not Pass' signs hanging on the wall of your comfort zone and charged on through regardless.

One of the most positive motivational speakers that America ever produced was Zig Ziglar. He would describe the start of his day in such a beautiful way. He used to say, 'Every morning at 6 am my opportunity clock would go off and wake me up. I don't call it an alarm clock because that's negative. That bell signals the start of a whole new day full of fantastic opportunities.'

IT'S NOT JUST YOU

The most important point I want you to take from this book, is this, perfection doesn't exist. We are all broken, just in different places. That might sound depressing but in reality it is beautiful. Once you understand that perfection does not exist then you can see that the beauty is actually in the things we label as bad. If were all clones of the perfect human being then there could be no such thing as beauty. For something to exist there needs to be something else to compare it to. Imagine for me an airplane in the sky, flying at 600 miles per hour. Now take away the sky, the clouds, the horizon, the earth, take away everything apart from the plane itself. Now the plane may still be flying at the same speed but it will now no longer appear to be moving at all. Without something to compare it to then the thing we marvel at does not exist at all.

The self-doubt you feel is an illusion because you are taking a fluid viewpoint and assuming it is a solid fact. Let me give you an example of what I mean. About three years ago I rescued a dog, that I eventually called Laika. She is a pointer cross, a hunting dog who is unfortunately afraid of loud noises. Which is a bit like being an airline pilot who is afraid of heights. Despite being entirely unsuitable for her calling, you will never meet a more affectionate animal; her soul is made from pure love and it pours out of her in bucket loads. However, because she was considered a failure as a hunting dog she was badly beaten and dumped on the side of a highway. In the last few years I have made a note of how friends and family have described her:

- *No offence but she is not going to win any beauty contests.*

- *Oh my God she is so beautiful*

- *She's a lovely dog but she not a good-looking dog.*

- *Your dog is beautiful; I have totally fallen in love with her.*

So which is she, ugly or beautiful? To me she is the latter but to other people whose opinions I respect she is also ugly. What this means is that Laika's physical appearance is not a solid thing, it is fluid and it changes depending on who is looking at her. The beauty is not in the thing we are looking at but we create it in our own mind. Believe it or not this doesn't just apply to animals. If you look in the mirror and say 'oh my God you are so ugly', you are correct. But conversely you can look in the same mirror, declare your earth shattering beauty and also be correct. My partner Daniela demonstrates this to me on a regular basis. Here in Cyprus we live in a very hot climate, which means we get a wide array of bugs and creepy crawlies sharing our world. Daniela can glance at the ugliest, most grotesque looking bug as it crawls across our doorstep and declare with total sincerity 'oh how beautiful it is'. I look the same thing and it appears to me as attractive as a bulldog that has ran into a wall at high speed. Of course I know she is right and I am wrong, but I am glad one of us can see the truth at least.

The next time you criticize yourself, I want you to ask yourself the question 'compared to what'. Look, I think I am a pretty intelligent guy but I also know that this is a fluid statement. If I compare myself to Stephen Hawking then boy, am I a dunce!

Or to give you another example: I think I am a handsome guy, but if you are asking how I compare to Tom Hardy, then I fully accept that I am not much better than the Elephant man. The good news is if we can twist the positive views of ourselves like that then we must also be able to twist the negative ones too. If you think you are too tall, ask yourself 'compared to what'. In a group of basketball players you would be called Shorty McShorty-Short!

Barrie's super honest Facebook post teaches us all something very important. We are not alone in our doubts and worries. There is not a single person alive on earth right now who is entirely comfortable with everything about themselves! What you really think Brad Pitt never looks in the mirror and says to himself 'jeez I look rough today". Do you really think J-Lo gets up every morning, looks at herself in the mirror and sees nothing but perfection? I can tell you that in the years I spent working as a wedding photographer, I discovered that it is the most beautiful people who seem to be the most critical of their looks. The slightest blemish is a huge problem, the truth is the feel the same as any other average looking person but just in a different way. Remember what I said earlier, we are all broken but just in different places.

I once shot the wedding of a professional swimwear model called Andrea, she was perhaps the most beautiful and flawless woman I have ever seen. She even looked beyond amazing in the scruffy t-shirt and jeans she wore for the planning meeting we held at a hotel near the venue a few days prior to the wedding. On the big day itself she looked earth shatteringly breathtaking. Everything was perfect, her make up, shoes and dress all worked together in perfect synchronicity to give her lucky husband to be a jaw dropping moment as she walked down the aisle to become his wife. Just as she was supposed to leave the room and get in the wedding car, she sat down on the edge of the bed and burst into the most uncontrollable fit of tears I have ever seen before or since. She cried uncontrollably for five minutes, sobbing so hard she couldn't tell any of her bridesmaids or her very worried looking father what was wrong. Eventually she calmed down enough to reveal what had brought her to such devastation. She looked at her sister, who was one of the bridesmaids and said 'I look terrible! I hate my hair; I hate the way they have done my make up. I feel like I am the ugliest I have ever been, and today I should be the most beautiful'.

As you would expect, everyone in that room rushed to assure Andrea that she was beautiful, including me. But it didn't make any difference, because the problem was not whether she was beautiful or not. The problem is not an external issue; it was entirely the program that is running in her head. And the same is true of everything you currently worry and stress about.

If there are things about yourself that you don't like then you have two choices. You can take action and change them or if they can't be changed then you can decide to let go of the denial and embrace them as a part of you. Stop beating yourself up because you have the occasionally anxiety attack when life gets tough. Stop hating yourself because you panic whenever you are asked to speak in public. You can't defeat problems by pretending they are not there, just like an alcoholic will never get better until he or she first admits that they have a problem. If you are overweight then grab a hold of your flab and shout out "I am a fatty", be the most confident fat person you ever met. It might sound counter intuitive and perhaps even crazy to suggest you embrace the very things that are making you miserable, but you should trust me on this. Unless you make friends with your problems they will always fight against you.

If you want to win and unleash your full potential you first have to accept the situation as it is right now. If you are in a crappy relationship stop pretending you are not. Embrace it, there is no failure only feedback. So, now you know the sort of relationship you don't want – be thankful for the lesson, no matter how painful it has been. Next you need to go after what you want to replace this situation with. It's not going to be easy but there is a simple system to ensure you reach your goal. Never give up, no matter how many times you get knocked down get up one more time.

Forget about positive thinking, education and good old-fashioned hard work. The secret to an exceptional life is persistence. Once you have determined precisely what it is you want to accomplish, you must take massive action on a consistent, persistent basis to succeed. Think of it like building a muscle. If you have ever weight trained before, the first time you walk into a gym, chances are you will not be able to bench press 250 lbs. However, if you are persistent, and you consistently go back to the gym, you will find yourself getting stronger and closer to your goal with every visit.

One of the things you'll notice on your journey towards your goal is roadblocks. That is, you will encounter obstacles that seem to jump out of nowhere in an attempt to halt your progress. Count on these obstacles. They are a part of life. Everyone would have all success they ever wanted if there were no obstacles. Your job is to be persistent and work through those obstacles. If you find little or no obstacles along the way, chances are you are not challenging yourself. And when you do reach your goal, you won't experience the feeling of 'sweet success.' Make your goal a challenging one!

If you take the time to study any successful person, you will learn that the vast majority of them have had more 'failures' than they have had 'successes.' This is because successful people are persistent; the more they stumble and fall, the more they get right back up and get going again. On the other hand, people that don't get back up and try again, never reach success. For example, Walt Disney was turned down 302 times before he got financing for his dream of creating the "Happiest Place on Earth." Today, due to his persistence, millions of people have shared 'the joy of Disney.' Colonel Sanders spent two years driving across the United States looking for restaurants to buy his chicken recipe. He was turned down 1,009 times! How successful is Kentucky Fried Chicken today?

Having said this, keep in mind that you must constantly re-evaluate your circumstances and the approach you are using to reach your goal. There is no sense in being persistent at something that you are doing incorrectly! Sometimes you have to modify your approach along the way. Every time you do something you learn from it, and therefore find a better way to do it the next time.

Today is the day to begin your journey, using consistency and persistence, towards tomorrow's successes!

In this world there are drivers and passengers. Or putting it another way, people who never stop moving forward and people who quit and get carried along by the wake – constantly tossed around and abused by the swell of life. One of the most common causes of failure is the habit of quitting when one is overtaken by temporary defeat. Every person is guilty of this mistake at one time or another.

An uncle of R.U. Darby was caught by the "gold fever" in the gold-rush days and went west to DIG AND GROW RICH. He had never heard that more gold had been mined from the brains of men than has ever been taken from the earth. He staked a claim and went to work with pick and shovel. The going was hard, but his lust for gold was definite.

After weeks of labor, he was rewarded by the discovery of the shining ore. He needed machinery to bring the ore to the surface. Quietly, he covered up the mine, retraced his footsteps to his home in Williamsburg, Maryland, told his relatives and a few neighbors of the "strike." They got together money for the needed machinery, had it shipped. The uncle and Darby went back to work the mine.

The first car of ore was mined and shipped to a smelter. The returns proved they had one of the most productive mines in Colorado! A few more cars of that ore would clear the debts. Then would come the big killing in profits.

Down went the drills! Up went the hopes of Darby and Uncle! Then something happened! The vein of gold ore disappeared! They had come to the end of the rainbow, and the pot of gold was no longer there! They drilled on, desperately trying to pick up the vein again – all to no avail.

Finally, they decided to QUIT.

They sold the machinery to a junk man for a few hundred dollars and took the train back home. Some "junk" men are dumb, but not this one! He called in a mining engineer to look at the mine and do a little calculating. The engineer advised that the project had failed because the owners were not familiar with "fault lines." His calculations showed that the vein would be found JUST THREE FEET FROM WHERE THE DARBYS HAD STOPPED DRILLING! That is exactly where it was found!

The "Junk" man took millions of dollars in ore from the mine because he knew enough to seek expert counsel before giving up.

Most of the money which went into the machinery was procured through the efforts of R.U. Darby, who was then a very young man. The money came from his relatives and neighbors, because of their faith in him. He paid back every dollar of it, although he was years in doing so.

Long afterward, Mr. Darby recouped his loss many times over, when he discovered that DESIRE can be transmuted into gold. The discovery came after he went into the business of selling life insurance.

Remembering that he lost a vast fortune because he STOPPED three feet from gold, Darby profited by the experience in his chosen work. he did this by saying to himself, "I stopped three feet from gold, but I will never stop because men say 'no' when I ask them to buy insurance."

Darby is one of a small group of fewer than fifty men who sell more than a million dollars in life insurance annually. He owes his "stickability" to the lesson he learned from his "quitability" in the gold mining business.

Before success comes in any man's life, he is sure to meet with much temporary defeat, and, perhaps, some failure. When defeat overtakes a man, the most natural and most logical thing to do is to QUIT. That is precisely what the majority of men do. This is what the passengers on the train nearly always do.

More than five hundred of the most successful men in the world, claim their greatest success came just one step beyond the point at which defeat had overtaken them. Failure is a trickster with a keen sense of irony and cunning. It takes great delight in tripping one when success is almost within reach.

SECTION FIVE – BECOMING A MASTER COMMUNICATOR

THE POWER OF YOUR WORDS

"Words - so innocent and powerless as they are, as standing in a dictionary, how potent for good and evil they become in the hands of one who knows how to combine them", Nathaniel Hawthorne

It's all well and good having a dream, but unless you can harness the power of other people, you will struggle to get there on your own. Your ability to communicate, persuade and motivate other people is a not only important. I would say that your level of skill in this area is the glass ceiling on your potential success.

When I talk about communication I am not just referring to the words we vocalize, for they are just the visible tip of the communication iceberg. People don't buy from salesmen purely based on the words he or she uses. Indeed, they could make the most convincing, articulately presented pitch and yet if the prospect finds something objectionable about the person making the pitch they will refuse to part with their hard-earned cash. We constantly make judgments and opinions of people with extremely limited data and often no proof at all to back up our presumptions. For example, if your prospect gets the impression that you are not to be trusted then you are going to face an extremely hard uphill climb ahead of you.

This subject is so important that I have a complete coaching program dedicated to it. You can find out more about my

Persuasion University course at www.CraigBeck.com. For this book we are going to merely brush the surface of this powerful and fascinating subject, to whet your appetite. Unstoppable people understand that good communication skills are crucial components of the art of persuasion. You need to understand how to persuade and influence in order to effectively motivate people into helping you to hit your targets. Now, please don't mistake the word 'persuasion' for the word 'manipulation'. The latter comes from a purely selfish and negative place and just like integrity or rather the lack of it. You can get to the top with manipulation but you won't stay there for long. Remember, you can get everything in life you want while you are busy giving other people what they want. Manipulation is a technique without balance and the universe will eventually forcibly correct this disharmony with an intensity equal to the level of its use.

The art of persuasion is a subtle comprehension of how people generate emotions based on material, intellectual and non-physical data. Emotions are the driving force behind all our actions. We don't want a diamond ring because it will look nice on our finger but rather how owning and wearing the ring will make us feel. I am writing this section of the book on a British Airways flight from London Heathrow to Larnaca, Cyprus. I have paid a premium to sit in the business class cabin. However, I am acutely aware that on paper that decision makes no financial sense at all. British Airways Club Europe seats are exactly the same as the economy seats, there is not a single extra inch of legroom and yet the price for a ticket is three times that of standard. I am not flying business because it's good value, but rather how it makes me feel. I like getting on the plane first, I like eating my meal off china table wear and I like getting off the plane first. From the viewpoint of value for money British Airways are laughing all the way to the bank. But they know that people buy with their emotions not with logic.

Learning how and why we generate emotions means that we can help people share our vision and help us move quickly toward our goals. Over ninety percent of our communication is non-verbal, that's why there is an entire course dedicated to the subject. So in this chapter, we will deal briefly with the tip of the iceberg only. Everyone knows that having a broad vocabulary is hugely beneficial but not all those words have equal value. Indeed two words that both mean the same thing can lead to vastly different outcomes when used in communication with others.

We call these 'power' words or 'trigger' words. A power word automatically calls an emotion from the subconscious. These are words like love, pain, desire, loss, money, mother, father, death.

These words can be used to significant effect in your presentation and your persuasion techniques, but use them with respect. They're not to be thrown away. They work best when delivered in a slightly different tone to the rest of your dialogue. You'll find ways to use these verbal anchors by always being aware of your prospects' environment. There will be traces of their private lives and personality in their office, in their car, in the way they dress, everywhere around them.

If a salesperson turns up to see a client and notices that he has a baby seat in the back of his car, you can be pretty sure what the most essential thing in their life is. Once you know what turns them on, what motives them, what triggers emotion in them, you can make compelling presentations to them.

Here's an example of a power word in use. Imagine our salesman walks into a client's office, and he notices on the desk there's a silver-framed picture of a child of the age of about two years old. Now, he could show an interest by saying 'oh is that your kid,' but, as any loving parent will tell you, the better way to say it would be 'oh is that your baby.' The word baby automatically generates an emotion. It's an anchor word. The kid is just a word. It's a throwaway.

In the same way, certain words are embedded as emotion calling trigger words. Even specific tones of voice or ways of speaking can recall feelings. I don't know about you, but my mother had a tone of voice that filled me with dread. I only had to hear 'Craig!' bellowing out, and I'd think 'oh my God, what have I done now?'. If it were horrible, I'd get my full name mentioned. She would stand in the kitchen and shout, 'Craig David Beck, get down here now!'.

The entertainer and circus owner, P T Barnum, knew the best way to please a crowd of people was to make every one of them think the show was being produced just for them. He was looked on by most people as a lovable rogue, but others saw him as a manipulator and a swindler. He designed a way of creating sentences that appeared to be directly relevant to every person he met - so he could say them to people, and they would be astonished as to how he knew them so well having never met before.

These lines became known as 'Barnum statements, ' and they still work today. Psychics and fortune tellers have been using them to con willing fools for many years. Let me show you some examples of Barnum statements, statements that appear to be purely relevant to you but are relevant to everyone. You may have seen some of these if you read your daily horoscope in the newspaper.

- You have a high need for other people to like and admire you

- You pride yourself as an independent thinker, and you don't accept other people's statements without satisfactory proof.

- At times you're extroverted and sociable while at

different times you're introverted and wary;

- You find it unwise to be too frank and revealing yourself to others.

- On the outside, you seem to be pretty tough and hard but on the inside you're soft, and you have feelings too.

I am not suggesting you use Barnum statements, but I do want you to be aware of when they're being used on you. They're statements designed to make a lot of people feel special, but remember, it's a trick. It could be the forerunner for a heavy sales pitch. Don't fall into the trap of Barnum statements.

We couldn't talk about emotions without talking about the two biggest ones, pleasure and pain. These two are such powerful motivators that some people believe everything we do, everything we have ever done, has been purely in the avoidance of pain and the achievement of pleasure.

Some psychologists theorize that we will do more to avoid pain than we will do to gain pleasure. However, I believe the concept is more complex than that. If that were true, then anyone who went on a diet would succeed, but the reality is that research shows us that ninety-five percent of people who go on a diet within two years have not only put back on the weight that they lost but an extra two pounds as well. Ninety-five percent is a pretty startling number, and I believe it has a lot to do with the pleasure/pain motivation versus time.

You see, if you're overweight, the pain is that you feel fat, unattractive and unhealthy. You have low self-esteem, you can't always shop in the shops you want to for the clothes you want. You can't keep up with your young children. You feel sluggish and tired all the time. There's a whole pile of pain in this situation. So to try and get away from the pain you go on a diet.

The problem is with a diet is the time it takes to move from pain to pleasure is pretty substantial, especially if you are, say, fifty pounds overweight. The weight will not come off overnight. It could take a year or more before you reach your target, before you reach your pleasure goal. Since it takes so long to move away from the pain, people get depressed and fed up with the diet and then along comes a chocolate bar.

Now, the difference with a chocolate bar is that the pleasure is instant. You open the wrapper, you smell the milk chocolate, and you taste the sugar and the cocoa beans. The energy rushes through your body, the endorphins are released, and you get your reward instantly. If you had a chocolate bar or any other food that's tasty (but considered unhealthy), and you had to wait six months for the taste and feelings to come, how many people in the world would be overweight? I don't think it would be many.

Bearing this principle in mind, during your persuasion conversation with someone, remember that if you can show them by doing what you are suggesting they will move quickly away from pain or promptly towards pleasure, you will have one very willing prospect.

For example, a pharmacist could say to a patient with a severe cough, 'yeah, sure, that cough medicine you've selected will certainly help. In fact, it's one of our best-selling lines. It should have your cough cleared up in around three days. Mind you if you'd like something a bit more effective then you should try this product. It's a little bit more expensive, but everyone who has tried it so far says their cough has been gone by the morning'. Which one would you go for?

Another set of automatic anchors in every one of us are triggered by the way our body moves or the action we take with it. The most potent example of this is a smile. The act of smiling causes the body and mind to act accordingly. Try it. Smile your biggest smile. Laugh out loud. Hold your head high and put your shoulders back and smile. Now try not to feel happy. Try moaning and complaining in your head but without letting the smile drop. It's tough to do. The action of smiling is a heavily repeated and embedded trigger.

Over your life to date, every time you've been in an intensely happy state, you've smiled at the same time. So if you want to feel satisfied just smile, a real smile, not just showing your teeth to the world. Feel it. If you stand tall with your head held high, eyes wide open, breathing firmly and sincerely, you get an almost instant rush of confidence, as opposed to if you're just slumped in your chair head down, softly breathing.

If you can, try jumping into the air and punching the air and shouting yes! Now try doing it while feeling miserable. It's virtually impossible. These psychological anchors are so embedded, they control the way you feel when you use them. Again, this is a bonus for the master communicator, since this rule applies to everyone you speak to.

If you're not driving in your car right now, try this anchor with me. This one uses nothing more than your breathing. I just want to show you that by doing a particular thing with your body you can induce a feeling of relaxation; only by doing one thing. All I want you to do is slow down your breathing. I want you to find that your breathing matches mine. I want you to take a big breath in now and hold it. Breathe out and breathe in, a big breath in and breathe out and just keep going at this pace, breathing in and holding it and breathing out.

Notice how your body relaxes of its own accord. Your muscles loosen, thoughts slow down, and you just automatically relax, purely and simply by altering your breathing. Finally for this chapter, I would like to give you my ten key qualities of the master communicator.

Number one - understand that human beings at their very core are good-intentioned people. Humans do not enjoy negativity.

They don't seek out pain or suffering. They may accidentally move people around them into that stage while trying to move away from it, but they don't intend to do it.

People can be kind and loving, supporting, but also, at the same time, manipulative, violent and obnoxious. They don't manifest these negative traits for the sake of it, or because they hate you or even because they enjoy being obnoxious. We are, as a general rule, all good people who happen to be driven by our needs.

Whatever communication you're in, whether it's a pleasant one or an aggressive one, remember everyone is trying to move some part of their situation away from pain and towards pleasure. If you can help them do that, you will get what you want as a natural by-product of that action.

Number two - believe there is no such thing as failure, only outcomes. Everything that has happened before has served to bring you where you are today, and for that, you should be grateful. Tomorrow is always an exciting new day. Remember, it took Thomas Edison 10,000 attempts to create the electric light bulb - 9,999 versions did not work, but he would never have got to success, version 10,000 without the other 9,999 outcomes to learn from.

Number three - become a perspective shifter; step into the other person's shoes. We all see things perfectly clearly from our point of view, but to understand the situation better, just pause to consider the conversation as it sounds in the other person's head.

Number four - understand the power of emotions. Be aware that our minds and bodies are as one. Powerful emotions can be triggered in a multitude of ways, from the smell of a familiar perfume to a hug from a friend to the kind words whispered from a colleague. Emotions are extremely powerful things.

Number five - continually review your approach. What works for one person may not work for another. Tailor your communication to every person you meet and, if your plan is not working, be ready to change it in an instant. Don't keep pounding forward, assuming they will give in and see your point of view eventually. If you speak French to someone who can only speak German, you can shout and scream as long as you want but they will never get to the point where they understand what you want until you change your approach.

Number six - expect success in everything you do. If you're trying to get a new job, act in your head like you already have it. Remember the subconscious cannot distinguish fact from fantasy. Believe you are rich, and the subconscious will go all out to deliver that to you.

The funniest and most ridiculous statement you will ever hear anyone say is 'oh, I always expect the worst to happen so then I can't be disappointed.' I still laugh when I hear people say that. They do have no idea that they are subconsciously programming every aspect of their life for failure. What a disaster.

Number Seven - understand why avoiding negatives are so significant in everything you do. The brain has real trouble with negatives and often gives you the opposite result as to what you wanted. Remember what happens when someone says to you 'whatever you do, don't look over there now.'

Number eight - remember that you finish school, but you never finish learning. Subscribe to the theory of the automobile university. Listen to educational, motivational and success audio products in your car every day. Surround yourself with successful people and their books, tapes, and videos.

Stay away from those negative people who expect failure and would prefer you to fail too so that they have some company at the bottom. Remember, if you lie down with dogs you will get up with fleas, so aim for the top and shrug off the people who try and convince you to stay where you are and as you are. Think of life as a triangle. Aim to be one of the people at the top. It's less crowded there, and the view is fantastic.

Number nine - always go for the win, win situation with everyone you meet. The best salesman in the world will only sell a product to people if they firmly believe they will have a better life because of it. People who sell anything to anyone, regardless of whether or not it will fulfill a need for that person are not a salesman, they are conmen. You may see them reach the top, but they'll be there on their own, and their journey back down is a certainty.

The best salesmen only sell products they firmly believe in and use themselves. If sales is your chosen career, ask yourself this question: 'would you sell your products to your close family and friends?'. If the answer is no, then your products are not good enough for your family and friends and, subsequently, they're not good enough for your customers. Get a different job or a different product. Never approach any sale or persuasion with your reward in mind. You get what you want as a by-product of giving other people what they want, not the other way around.

Number ten for the master communicator - understand what the most critical word in the whole world is. You know the English language is a beautiful thing. Playwrights and poets can reduce you to tears or fill you with joy, just by the way they construct words on a page. Generals can motivate an army to die for their country by the way they communicate their passion for victory and freedom.

However, there is just one word, one word in the whole world that stands head and shoulders above the rest, regardless of language, dialect, tone, intonation. Only one word that creates a powerful instant emotion in a person. That word is their name.

A person's name is a beautiful thing to them. It's one of the first words they ever learn. It's what their friends, relatives, husbands, and wives call them. When you say their first name, you massage the most active, most deep-rooted desire found in every person on earth, the need to feel important. By proving you remember their name, you're saying you are important enough to me to remain in my memory, and I care about you.

I challenge you here and now to experiment with those most basic of concepts. For example, next time you're walking to work, go up to the receptionist and smile and say 'good morning, Jean, how are you?'. I know that you will get a much brighter response than the day before when you gave her a simple, non-personal greeting.

KNOW YOUR TYPE

Have you ever wondered how someone could look at the same situation as you and feel entirely different about it? Perhaps you are the sort of person who likes to turn up at the airport and catch the first available flight you find. Life is an adventure to you and surprises, and unforeseen challenges add to the enjoyment. However, you invite your friend to come on vacation, but they want to carefully research every possible location, check the exchange rates and precisely plan every moment of your trip to ensure maximum value for money. Your friend may think you are sloppy, lazy and ill-prepared but you may judge your friend to be sucking all the fun out of what was supposed to be an exciting idea. Neither person is right, and yet neither person is wrong - it's just that we are all wired differently.

I fundamentally believe that your level of success today has a great deal to do with how well you understand and communicate with other people. It's very easy to observe someone else's behavior and label it weird or wrong because it doesn't fit with how we do things. For example, my wife finds me infuriating at times because in a lot of areas of our personality we directly oppose each other. I am a creative, big picture thinker - I see the vision, and I want to charge ahead and manifest it. Whereas Daniela is a detail person, she needs to ensure all the T's are crossed and all the I's are correctly dotted before we move onto the next phase. This is great for her because it serves her well in her role as an accountant. However, ask her how she feels about the way I do laundry, and her head will explode.

I am sure you can imagine that this conflict of personality

can potentially cause huge problems in relationships. Perhaps you have ended relationships with people with using an explanation such as 'they just didn't get you' or 'they had no consideration for how I felt'. Without an understanding of the sixteen different personality types, you may end up labeling these people somewhere between weird and evil. The contrast between Daniela and I could easily have destroyed our relationship but for one thing. Awareness, we understand each other at a deep psychological level. I love that my wife sees the world in an entirely different way. Sometimes I feel like a blind man, and she has her hand on my arm guiding down a path I don't recognize. I am what is know as an INFP personality type (my wife is an ISTJ), and I understand that as such I have some fantastic gifts in my arsenal but I am also aware of where I am weak. In situations where I am being forced to act in one of my secondary skillsets I always ask my wife for help and advice. What's more, I always make sure I listen to her because I am acutely aware that she can see the situation in a full spectrum of colors whereas to me it looks black and white.

I have no doubt that you have avoided people and ended relationships purely because neither of you understood the personality traits of the other. You both concluded that the other person was selfish, weird and awkward. The truth is it was the blind leading the blind. There is no point using outlandish, loud and brash communication with an introverted personality type they are just going to label you a loud mouth who talks but never listens.

At the QUIT DRINKING BOOTCAMP event everyone gets to find out what personality type they are but for now let me give you a rough outline of the sixteen types:

The Inspector – ISTJ Personality

At first glance, ISTJs are intimidating. They appear serious, formal, and proper. They also love traditions and old-school values that uphold patience, hard work, honor, and social and cultural responsibility. They are reserved, calm, quiet, and upright. These traits result from the combination of I, S, T, and J, a personality type that is often misunderstood.

INFJ Personality

INFJs are visionaries and idealists who ooze creative imagination and brilliant ideas. They have a different, and usually more profound, way of looking at the world. They have a substance and depth in the way they think, never taking anything at surface level or accepting things the way they are. Others may sometimes perceive them as weird or amusing because of their different outlook on life.

The Mastermind – INTJ Personality

INTJs, as introverts, are quiet, reserved, and comfortable being alone. They are usually self-sufficient and would rather work alone than in a group. Socializing drains an introvert's energy, causing them to need to recharge. INTJs are interested in ideas and theories. When observing the world they are always questioning why things happen the way they do. They excel at developing plans and strategies and don't like uncertainty.

ENFJs are people-focused individuals. They are extroverted, idealistic, charismatic, outspoken, highly principled and ethical, and usually know how to connect with others no matter their background or personality. Mainly relying on intuition and feelings, they tend to live in their imagination rather than in the real world. Instead of focusing on living in the "now" and what is currently happening, ENFJs tend to concentrate on the abstract and what could happen in the future.

The Craftsman – ISTP Personality
ISTPs are mysterious people who are usually very rational and logical, but also quite spontaneous and enthusiastic. Their personality traits are less easily recognizable than those of

other types, and even people who know them well can't always anticipate their reactions. Deep down, ISTPs are spontaneous, unpredictable individuals, but they hide those traits from the outside world, often very successfully.

The Provider – ESFJ Personality

ESFJs are the stereotypical extroverts. They are social butter-flies, and their need to interact with others and make people happy usually ends up making them popular. The ESFJ usually tends to be the cheerleader or sports hero in high school and college. Later on in life, they continue to revel in the spotlight and are primarily focused on organizing social events for their families, friends, and communities. ESFJ is a common personality type and one that is liked by many people.

The Idealist – INFP Personality

INFPs, like most introverts, are quiet and reserved. They prefer not to talk about themselves, especially in the first encounter with a new person. They like spending time alone in quiet places where they can make sense of what is happening around them. They love analyzing signs and symbols and consider them to be metaphors that have deeper meanings related to life. They are lost in their imagination and daydreams, always drowned in the depth of their thoughts, fantasies, and ideas.

The Performer – ESFP Personality

ESFPs have an Extraverted, Observant, Feeling and Perceiving personality, and are commonly seen as Entertainers. Born to be in front of others and to capture the stage, ESFPs love the spotlight. ESFPs are thoughtful explorers who love learning and sharing what they learn with others. ESFPs are "people people" with strong interpersonal skills. They are lively and fun and enjoy being the center of attention. They are warm, generous, and friendly, sympathetic and concerned about other people's well-being.

The Champion – ENFP Personality

ENFPs have an Extraverted, Intuitive, Feeling and Perceiving personality. This personality type is highly individualistic, and Champions strive toward creating their methods, looks, actions, habits, and ideas — they do not like cookie cutter people and hate when they are forced to live inside a box. They like to be around other people and have a strong intuitive nature when it comes to themselves and others. They operate from their feelings most of the time, and they are highly perceptive and thoughtful.

The Doer – ESTP Personality

ESTPs have an Extraverted, Sensing, Thinking, and Perceptive personality. ESTPs are governed by the need for social interaction, feelings, and emotions, logical processes and reasoning, along with a need for freedom. Theory and abstracts don't keep ESTP's interested for long. ESTPs leap before they look, fixing their mistakes as they go, rather than sitting idle or preparing contingency plans.

The Supervisor – ESTJ Personality

ESTJs are organized, honest, dedicated, dignified, traditional, and are great believers of doing what they believe is right and socially acceptable. Though the paths towards "good" and "right" are difficult, they are glad to take their place as the leaders of the pack. They are the epitome of good citizenry. People look to ESTJs for guidance and counsel, and ESTJs are always happy that they are approached for help.

The Commander – ENTJ Personality

An ENTJ's primary mode of living focuses on external aspects, and all things are dealt with rationally and logically. Their secondary mode of operation is internal, where intuition and reasoning take effect. ENTJs are natural born leaders among the

16 personality types and like being in charge. They live in a world of possibilities, and they often see challenges and obstacles as great opportunities to push themselves. They seem to have a natural gift for leadership, making decisions, and considering options and ideas quickly yet carefully. They are "take charge" people who do not like to sit still.

The Thinker – INTP Personality

INTPs are well known for their brilliant theories and unrelenting logic, which makes sense since they are arguably the most logical minded of all the personality types. They love patterns, have a keen eye for picking up on discrepancies, and an excellent ability to read people, making it a bad idea to lie to an INTP. People of this personality type aren't interested in practical, day-to-day activities and maintenance, but when they find an environment where their creative genius and potential can be expressed, there is no limit to the time, and energy INTPs will expend in developing an insightful and unbiased solution.

The Nurturer – ISFJ Personality

ISFJs are philanthropists, and they are always ready to give back and return generosity with even more kindness. The people and things they believe in will be upheld and supported with enthusiasm and unselfishness. ISFJs are warm and kind-hearted. They value harmony and cooperation and are likely to be very sensitive to other people's feelings. People appreciate the ISFJ for their consideration and awareness, and their ability to bring out the best in others.

The Visionary – ENTP Personality

Those with the ENTP personality are some of the rarest in the world, which is entirely understandable. Although they are extroverts, they don't enjoy small talk and may not thrive in many social situations, especially those that involve people who are too different from the ENTP. ENTPs are intelligent and knowledgeable need to be constantly mentally stimulated. They can discuss theories and facts in extensive detail. They are logical, rational, and objective in their approach to information and arguments.

The Composer – ISFP Personality

ISFPs are introverts that do not seem like introverts. It is because even if they have difficulties connecting to other people at first, they become warm, approachable, and friendly eventually. They are fun to be with and very spontaneous, which makes them the perfect friend to tag along in whatever activity, regardless of planned or unplanned. ISFPs want to live their life to the fullest and embrace the present, so they make sure they are always out to explore new things and discover new experiences. It is through experience that they find wisdom, so they do see more value in meeting new people than other introverts.

Understanding personality type is hugely important because if you recognize more about the people you are interacting with, then you can tailor your communication style to their preferred way of receiving the message. Remember what Zig Ziglar said 'You can get everything in life that you want if you will just help enough other people to get what they want.' For example, let's say you are a car salesman and I walk into your showroom. You are an unconscious ESPF type; I don't mean you are passed out on the floor. Rather, you have no knowledge of personality types, and you assume that everyone thinks and feels like you do. If you approach me as an introverted INFP and throw an arm around my shoulder as you guide me around the car, excitedly raving about all its amazing features. You are not going to make a commision that day. I will feel like you were pushy, over the top salesman who didn't 'get me.' However, if another ESPF came into the showroom seconds later they would probably leave describing the same salesman as 'what a lovely guy.'

When there is a clash of personality in your social life, you can avoid the other person or end the relationship. However, where you don't have this option in your career and professional life. If your new boss is a conflicting personality type you can't just ignore and avoid him, well, you can, but it's not going to end well. If you are in business for yourself you cannot choose to only work with compatible personality types, as lovely as that would feel - it's just not possible. So, the only option is to learn and adapt to meet the needs of other people better. Can you see how awesomely valuable this knowledge is? If you are currently a salesman who does not use this knowledge and has a sales conversion rate of 15%, can you imagine what will happen to your income if you start tailoring your communication to match the client?

HOW TO DEAL WITH DIFFICULT PEOPLE

Have you ever had a meeting with someone and the more you talked, the angrier and less co-operative they became? You felt frustrated because you had some fantastic points to make and you genuinely believed you could add value to their life. However, for every great statement you made, they had an objection. These are the people we label as 'difficult' and they are everywhere. You will know friends who are 'difficult', co-workers and maybe even members of your family. If you have ever had to deal with a stroppy teenager, you will understand precisely what I am talking about. What you have to be aware of is, despite how it appears they are not 'bad' people or doing it to make your life difficult deliberately. They are what we call internal thinkers; they are taking the vast majority of their data from themselves. This means that they don't much care for your opinion and the fact that you are all flowery and creative with the information they don't need irritates them beyond belief.

I believe we see this 'difficult' streak in teenagers because they switch from needing the advice and guidance of their parents to wanting to be independent. I used to get so frustrated trying to help my daughter when she turned 13 years old. She would point blank ignore me, insisting that she knew better. I tried to use the logic that only one of us in the conversation has the experience of being 13 years old before, but it just made her behave more obnoxiously. Most teenagers grow out of this phase, some quickly and others it takes a painfully long time.

The difficult people you meet, who you may end up labeling as 'just an asshole', in reality are probably no different to you. They are just expressing themselves differently and are closed to external input. We all have areas where this holds true. For example the US at the moment you will find people furious at the presidency of Donald Trump. However, you will also find equally passionate and vocal people who think he's doing a great job. If you put these two sorts of people in the same room it is highly unlikely they are going to leave as friends. Neither party wants to listen to the other side, they are too firmly dug in to their own internal position.

The same is true in the UK around the thorny subject of Brexit. Many people, myself included are extremely against the prospect of the United Kingdom leaving Europe. We see as a illogical decision born out of low level racism and stupidity. Sadly, if you put a pro Brexit support in the same room as a 're-mainer' there is going to be trouble. You can't change someone's mind by telling them that they are wrong. This issue even exists in my own family. My father is a pro Brexiteer, if ask him to defend his position the veins in his neck start to swell even before he starts speaking. When I listen to him speak on the matter I feel that 99% of what he believes in nonsense. If he wasn't my father I would probably just walk away and forever label him an 'asshole'. However, I know this man and the kind, caring soul that lays beneath. So, we simply don't talk about the subject, because I think we both know that we are never going to change the opinion of the other person.

So, how do you deal with a problematic person like this, some-one who has closed you down and doesn't want to listen to reason? The best thing you can do is ask them what they want. Don't flog a dead horse, dump the spiel and pretty presentation - they don't care. They are thinking internally and not looking for external input. The chances are they are only talking to you because they believe you might be able to serve a purpose. If you want results with 'difficult' people just cut the crap and ask them what problem they have that you can help alleviate. It may not be the way you prefer to communicate or do business, but you don't have to marry them, get in and get out and you will both end up a lot happier.

This approach has multiple layers of benefits. Firstly, it reduces the amount of time you have to spend with difficult people, it allows you to meet the needs of your client quickly and efficiently and it is a huge time saver. If you are a manager you will be acutely aware just how many time thieves there are about the place. They usually knock on your office door and start the dialogue with 'Have you got 5 minutes"? They are all set to vent about someone or something that has upset them. It never takes just 5 minutes and it sucks the positive out of you. Instead of letting them blow off steam at your expense, stop them dead in their tracks and simply ask 'what can I do to help you'? It disarms them and renders there pre-prepared spewing of venom obsolete at the same time.

DATING AFTER QUITTING DRINKING – HOW IS THAT SUPPOSED TO WORK?

Alcohol causes severe damage to relationships; that much is obvious. However, it also covers up problems and dysfunction in your relationship. When you quit drinking, you are faced with a choice, to repair the damage alcohol has done to your relationship or to address the issues that alcohol was making you avoid dealing with.

When I stopped drinking my marriage also came to an end. I am not saying that quitting drinking caused the collapse of my marriage. Instead it was a period in my life where I decided I needed to learn how to love myself. I dumped this poison out of my life; I lost some weight and started taking better care of myself. I also decided that I wasn't happy and needed to make some dramatic changes in my life.

The short story is, I ended up being sober and single for the first time in nearly two decades. Whether you are in a similar experienced position or young free and single it is natural to worry about how you date and avoid alcohol at the same time.

The good news is, while it appears that alcohol and dating are intrinsically linked. Dating without booze is much better and much more rewarding.

You may worry that you will be more nervous and less confident without a little glass of Dutch Courage but as I have previously explained: Alcohol doesn't make you confident it just makes you stupid. You are less risk adverse and likely to charge ahead not because you are braver but rather because your intellectual capacity has been compromised.

I also remember going on drunken dates. I would start the evening not being very attracted to the woman I was talking to. However, the more I drunk, the more attractive she became to me. Again that might sound like a benefit but imagine what happens the next morning when the booze has worn off.

On the flip side, ask yourself 'do you really think women are impressed by the drunken, slurring approaches of men who need alcohol before they can act'?

What I discovered, to my shock, was that some women refuse to date you when they find out that you don't drink alcohol. When you get rejected for this reason, it is easy to feel resentment toward your sobriety. This is a mistake because you have been saved from wasting your time dating an alcoholic.

Only fellow 'problem drinkers' will refuse to date a teetotaler. They know it would cause them huge psychological pain to be with this person. They would have to sneak drinks when the other person wasn't looking to try and portray their drinking as 'normal.'

If you want to make your life 1000% better, then your goal should be to be in a relationship with someone who drinks in moderation or, even better, not at all!

I was in a long-term relationship with a woman who had a drinking problem, and it broke my heart. While I was never tempted to join her, it hurt to see a bright and intelligent woman turn into a stupid, brainless zombie.

Today I am in a beautiful relationship. My wife Daniela drinks about two beers a year! That means we never have alcohol in the house, neither of us ever waste a weekend in bed suffering from a hangover, and we never upset each other with silly drunken mistakes.

Women Prefer Sober Guys

Forgive me if this answer is geared toward men, it's just written from my own personal experience.

Women who are looking for a long-term relationship have specific filters. They want a man of value who is a successful, reliable provider. I do not mean they are looking for a man to pay for their every whim just that he is mature and responsible enough to hold down a decent job and make her proud of him.

There are a couple of things that you can bring up on a first date that will set substantial alarm bells ringing in the mind of many women. It should go without saying that a relaxed view of infidelity is a big no-no. However, mention that you love to go to the casino or start every anecdote with "one time when I was drunk,' and she will have red flags all over the place.

Many women have experienced the pain of being in a relationship with an addict. They know that whether it's booze or gambling, it will ultimately lead to a dishonest and painful relationship.

Sober guys are more valuable!

Aesthetically there are many benefits to dating without alcohol too. The hard reality is, non-drinkers just look better. They take better care of themselves and invest more in their appearance. Drinkers spend most of their spare cash on booze. They look tired, blotchy, bloated and tend to be overweight.

Stop worrying about taking the alcohol out of dating. When you understand the truth behind the smokescreen, you will realize it's a massive benefit for everyone involved.

HOW DO YOU GET THE MINDSET TO STAY HAPPY AND SOBER FOR THE REST OF YOUR LIFE?

At the back of my house, there is a substantial multi-gym. It cost me a lot of money, and I hate it! I hate it with a passion, every day when I walk past it I swear profusely at it.

However, every day without fail, I spend forty minutes using it. I don't do it because I enjoy it or because I want to look like a muscle man. I use it because I understand the consequences of not using it and I recognize the benefits of putting the effort in.

I am nearly 45 years old, and I understand that the aches and pains I feel these days are only going to get worse if I don't take action. Nobody is going to fix this problem for me and excuses are going to get me nothing but permission to fail.

Quitting drinking requires the same determination, maturity, and focus. You can't half-heartedly stop drinking, you are either committed to this decision, or you are not.

I see a recurring theme in the Stop Drinking Expert Facebook group. Somebody will confess to a moment of weakness the night before and reveal that they fell off the wagon. This will be followed by a series of well-meaning and supportive comments expressing empathy and sympathy.

This is not helpful!

Doing this would be the same as me coming up with a daily excuse to not use the multi-gym and then looking for sympathy from Daniela when she comes home from work.

"Oh Daniela, it's so terrible. I wanted to use the multi gym but then I felt a bit sick and decided to sit in front of the TV instead of... how awful it's been for me"

Every day I think of an excuse not to exercise, and every day I have a choice as to whether I use the reason or I act like a grown up and do what is required of me.

Once you are outside the physical kick of the drug, which lasts a few weeks and no more, you are into the territory of psychological issues and anchors. This is no different to other choices that you make daily.

When you choose to drink (because let's be honest, it is your decision – nobody pours it into your mouth) you are choosing to be a victim. Taking the path of least resistance nearly always gets you a poor outcome.

Think about it... it would be easier to sit at home than to get up every morning and go to work. It would be easier for me to throw a sheet over the multi-gym and forget I ever bought the bloody thing and it would be easier to just pour the glass of wine and drink it.

But, would any of those choices benefit you in the long run?

Of course not! So this is where you have to take responsibility for making the right choice. You are entirely capable of doing this because you prove it in other areas on a daily basis.

I am not writing this to bully you or patronize you. I want to encourage you to get motivated about this part of your life. I firmly believe that if you want to quit, and more importantly 'stay quit' then you have to adopt a binary mindset about this.

Quitting drinking is easy; just don't put alcohol in your mouth... there you've done it. Staying quit is about the choices you make on an ongoing basis.

It's easier to make good decisions when you have useful data to base them upon.

For example: If your child asked if they could go on a school trip abroad, you wouldn't just say yes without first asking some crucial questions and doing a little research. Perhaps after speaking to the school and some other parents, if you were comfortable that it was safe and sensible, you may decide to allow your child the trip.

Quitting drinking is an essential decision in your life. So, make sure you have a head full of sound and correct information to allow you to make wise choices. When you get the temptation to have 'just one glass of wine' if you know for 100% certainty that the drug is going to disable your ability to make rational decisions and deliberately try to force you to drink more, then it is easy to make a choice that will serve you in a positive way.

I use the multi gym every day because I understand that only I can make the choices required to ensure I am fit, healthy and happy. Quitting drinking is the same; actually, it is the ultimate act of self-respect.

Of course, quitting an addictive drug is not easy. If it were easy, then I would not be writing this book. You will notice that there is no such website as stopeatingpeanutsexpert.com. You know why? Because if you start eating too many peanuts, you stop doing it – job done.

If you are serious about beating this problem, then you have to fight, and fight hard. Nobody is motivated to go to the gym because they love the equipment or because they enjoy getting changed back and forth into sweat pants. People go to a gym because they fall in love with the result of their effort, dedication, and determination.

Legendary boxer Mohammed Ali famously revealed that he hated every single second of training. However, he made a committed decision to ignore the short-term discomfort, in order to live the rest of his life as a champion. I encourage you to get the same eye of the tiger mentality. You must decide now to take on the Evil Clown and give him the fight of his life.

Float like a butterfly and sting like a bee.

Take ownership of this challenge, become obsessive about learning the truth about this drug and use the weight of this knowledge to help you make empowering decisions.

SECTION SIX – THE INTERVENTION

AN ATTITUDE OF GRATITUDE

Have an attitude of gratitude. This is a popular and perhaps over pronounced statement, but one can never underestimate the power behind these words. You may have heard the advice that in order to attract something you want you must act like you already have it. To give thanks as though that new car or lottery win is already in your possession.

As we have already discovered; focusing on what you don't want is futile. But also daydreaming of one day being slim or one day being rich is a self-defeating exercise. These dreams are all in the tomorrow, set in a time period that doesn't yet exist and as such are quite frankly none of your business. Concentrate on what is in your life today, this moment and be grateful for it. Even problems present as an opportunity for love and gratitude. Give your problems to divinity, ask the universe to erase them and then give thanks for that.

I think Marelisa Fabrega describes it best in her change blog when she says:

Gratitude means thankfulness, counting your blessings, noticing simple pleasures, and acknowledging everything that you receive. It means learning to live your life as if everything were a miracle, and being aware on a continuous basis of how much you've been given. Gratitude shifts your focus from what your life lacks to the abundance that is already present. In addition, behavioral and psychological research has shown the surprising life improvements that can stem from the practice of gratitude. Giving thanks makes people happier and more resilient, it strengthens relationships, it improves health, and it reduces stress.

Two psychologists, Michael McCollough of Southern Methodist University in Dallas, Texas, and Robert Emmons of the University of California at Davis, wrote an article about an experiment they conducted on gratitude and its impact on well-being. The study split several hundred people into three different groups and all of the participants were asked to keep daily diaries. The first group kept a diary of the events that occurred during the day without being told specifically to write about either good or bad things; the second group was told to record their unpleasant experiences; and the last group was instructed to make a daily list of things for which they were grateful. The results of the study indicated that daily gratitude exercises resulted in higher reported levels of alertness, enthusiasm, determination, optimism, and energy. In addition, those in the gratitude group experienced less depression and stress, were more likely to help others, exercised more regularly, and made greater progress toward achieving personal goals.

People tend to take for granted the good that is already present in their lives. There's a gratitude exercise that instructs that you should imagine losing some of the things that you take for granted, such as your home, your ability to see or hear, your ability to walk, or anything that currently gives you comfort. Then imagine getting each of these things back, one by one, and consider how grateful you would be for each and every one. In addition, you need to start finding joy in the small things instead of holding out for big achievements such as getting the promotion, having a comfortable nest egg saved up, getting married, having the baby, and so on–before allowing yourself to feel gratitude and joy.

Another way to use giving thanks to appreciate life more fully is to use gratitude to help you put things in their proper perspective. When things don't go your way, remember that every difficulty carries within it the seeds of an equal or greater benefit. In the face of adversity ask yourself: "What's good about this?", "What can I learn from this?", and "How can I benefit from this?"

Once you become oriented toward looking for things to be grateful for, you will find that you begin to appreciate simple pleasures and things that you previously took for granted. Gratitude should not be just a reaction to getting what you want, but an all-the-time gratitude, the kind where you notice the little things and where you constantly look for the good even in unpleasant situations. Today, start bringing gratitude to your experiences, instead of waiting for a positive experience in order to feel grateful; in this way, you'll be on your way toward becoming a master of gratitude.

Of course, having an attitude of gratitude sounds easy, but just like motivation and romance, it is not something that lasts forever without effort. My parents always used to say 'you have to work at your relationship', I would nod and agree, but in my head, I was thinking 'surely if you are in the right relationship it should just flow automatically.' It wasn't until I understood that nothing grows in your comfort zone and if you are not growing you are dying that I realized what they meant.

Daniela and I are very happy together, but we both know that if we relax too far into the relationship, we will lose the magic and start taking each other for granted. I understand that it's the little things I do that make her feel loved, not the big but infrequent gestures. I tell her she looks beautiful every day, no matter where I am in the world I say good morning and good night and I am always waiting at the gate when she comes home from work. It would be very easy to stop any one of those things, and most likely my relationship would carry on just fine, but it wouldn't be the same fantastic thing in my life. Having an attitude of gratitude is precisely the same, most people start very enthusiastic and committed but slowly their motivation fades, and without even being aware of it they find they have stopped all their grateful habits.

As much as I love my wife it does not mean I don't need reminders of what I should be doing. If you looked through my diary right now, you would see little entries in red. Questions such as 'what have you done for Daniela today'? I put those in my diary many years ago because I never wanted to lose sight of how important to me she is. I also came up with two powerful ways to keep my energy and direction focused on gratitude and love. The first is my daily journal, I will explain how it works, and you may be tempted to think that it's far too simple to make any real difference. Let me tell you that this simple daily routine has changed and enhanced my life more than anything else I have ever learned or done.

Every morning I sit down with a cup of coffee, and I open a very beautiful leather-bound notepad. Clipped to the side of this pad is a wonderfully elegant silver fountain pen. This daily diary is called my 421 Journal. If you are serious about changing your life, I suggest you do the same thing every day. Today go and buy a notepad and pen. I find it adds to the routine if you put a little care and attention into the writing materials you are going to be using. Buy a beautiful notebook and a pen that you like to write with. This routine is going to be an essential and magical part of your day, so make sure it feels significant.

The number 421 refers to the balance of giving, sending and receiving you are going to be offering to the universe every day. It is vital that you find a moment of peace and tranquility every day where you can do this. Your focus needs to be entirely on the page. If the children are running around the kitchen while you are trying to write or your secretary keeps calling you at your desk, then your attention is broken. For example, this morning I got up at 5:30 am, an hour before Daniela gets up for work. I fed the dogs and cats and made myself a cup of coffee. Then I sat in silence and opened my journal. I already knew what I was going to write because I had awoken a few times during the night with thoughts that I instantly decided needed to be in my diary for today.

At the top of a new page, I wrote today's date, 2nd December 2018. Next, I started to write out four statements of things in my life that I am profoundly grateful for. I woke up this morning next to the woman of my dreams. So the first line of my journal today states 'Thank you for the amazing, loving relationship that Daniela and I enjoy so much'.

Next, I write down two things in my awareness that need more love. I sent my love to my daughter, who is having a tough time at the moment, and also to a friend who today will have a biopsy on his lung to check for cancer.

Finally, I wrote down my intention for today, or if you prefer, my instruction to the universe of what I want to be delivered. This doesn't have to be an earth-shatteringly large request; it can be big or small. A steady stream of small manifestations is much more rewarding than taking risks with gigantic requests to win the lottery, etc. I have some good news and some bad news for you about this whole law of attraction thing. The bad news is that this is not Aladdin's lamp. You can't wish for anything and WHOOSH it magically appears. Imagine if ten thousand people bought this book and all on the same day they wrote 'I want to win the lottery today.' How can the universe generate that many winning tickets? And even if it did, the prize pool would be divided so many times that every single person would be left disappointed. You are asking the universe to push you in a direction rather than just hand stuff to you on a silver plate. If you ask to meet your soulmate, the universe will not create a new person from scratch (like in that movie Weird Science), but instead, it will start moving two compatible people closer together, motivating you both to be at the same place at the same time and so on.

The 421 Journal is designed to put your primary focus on giving rather than on receiving. Each day's entry starts with four expressions of gratitude for what you already have in your life, two gifts of love for someone else and one cosmic order to the universe. You will come to see this journal as something quite magical in your life, a sacred document. When I sit down to write in my own 421 Journal, I take the process very seriously. I make sure I am in a quiet place on my own, and before I put pen to paper, I sit in silent contemplation for a few moments. I know that what I write in that book will become a reality, so it is worth pausing just for a moment and focusing on what would serve me best. There is no doubt in my mind that what I have asked for will be delivered; I know that the moment the intention is set, the outcome has already happened—even before the ink dries. All I have to do next is wait patiently for time to catch up. It's a bit like sending an ethereal email—once you click submit you can't see where the message is on its journey, and you don't worry about which part of the Internet is currently hosting your communication. As soon as you click send an unbreakable chain of events begins. If you have ever sent an email to entirely the wrong (and most inappropriate) person, then you will know firsthand that it doesn't matter how many times you click cancel. That disastrous message has already delivered its payload.

Here is my full 421 journal entry for today:

Sunday 2nd December 2018

Gratitude

1.　Thank you for the amazing, loving relationship that Daniela and I enjoy so much.
2.　Thank you for the abundance in my life that opens so many beautiful windows of opportunity on a daily basis.
3.　Thank you for my abilities and opportunity to change and improve the lives of so many good people around the world.
4.　I am so grateful that I continue to learn and grow as a person.

Love

1.　I send my love to my daughter Aoife. May this new job bring her happiness, passion, and purpose. May it lead to many new and great things in her life.
2.　I send love to Mark, may the biopsy go just fine and the results be a cause for celebration.

Order

1.　Thank you for the great feedback, ratings, and reviews that I see appearing all over the Internet for this book.

Vision Board

The next thing I do every year is another one of those actions that are easily dismissed as too simple to make a difference. Especially if you are one of the personality types that needs a lot of data, facts, and proof before you can commit to something. In that case, you are just going to have to take a big leap of faith and trust me on this. In this book, I am giving you nothing but the good stuff, the things that I have used to transform my life and the lives of many millions of people around the world.

Vision boards work, and there's indeed a very basic explanation of the reason that they perform so good.

Making a sacred space that shows what you desire does bring it to life. What we concentrate on expands. When you make a vision board and place it in a place where you see it frequently, you effectively wind up performing brief visualization exercises across the working day.

Visualization is among the most effective mind exercises you can do. According to the well-known book The Secret, "The law of attraction is forging your complete life experience, and it is doing that via your thoughts and feelings. When you are visualizing, you are sending out a potent frequency out into the Universe."

Regardless if you believe that or otherwise, we understand that visualization works. Famous professional sportsmen have been using it for years to boost performance, and research has revealed that the brain sequences triggered when a weightlifter lifts heavy weights are also similarly triggered when the lifter simply thought of (visualized) lifting weights.

So, what's the big secret to making a vision board that works? It's straightforward: Your vision board ought to concentrate on how you wish to feel, not just on items that you desire. Don't get me wrong, it's fantastic to feature the material stuff, too. The more your board pays attention to how you wish to feel, the more it will come to life.

Here's an illustration. I have a British Airways 'First Class' luggage tag on my board. It's not that I aspire to always travel British Airways but rather I love flying, traveling and the comfort and experience of first class is the icing on the cake that makes the whole journey from start to finish amazing. It's how I always want to travel if I can, an indulgence I know, but it's something I love, and so it's on my board.

There is just one important rule to making a vision board that works, and it's that there aren't any rules. You aren't going to mess it up; you can develop your vision board on your terms. Here are the answers to the most typical questions folks ask:

Q: What should I place on my vision board?

A: Just about anything that motivates and encourages you. The function of your vision board is to deliver everything on it to life. Initially, consider what your objectives are in the following areas: romantic relationships, occupation, and resources, home, traveling, personal development (including spirituality, socializing, learning) and wellness.

You do not need to deal with each area precisely the same, take a personal inventory of what you wish each and every one of those parts to resemble and write them down. Always handwrite your objectives rather than typing them, there's something energized about literally handwriting your objectives. From your targets and goals, consider what you want on your vision board. Like I mentioned before, what you concentrate on expands. You'll be surprised at how things begin appearing everywhere as soon as you establish the intent for what you desire and how you wish to feel.

Q: Should I have just one primary vision board or many little ones for various parts of my lifestyle?

A: It's entirely up to you. What makes the most sense in your life? I like to have just one main vision board that I check out daily in my office, and I have a couple of little ones that I've created at retreats that I keep around too. Each part of our life-styles impact one another, so beginning with one main vision board typically makes good sense. Concept boards that focus on particular occasions or elements of your lifestyle are fantastic too, for example, a wedding-day-specific will assist you to concentrate on how you wish to feel on your wedding day, or a job specific board at your work desk space can help you work in the direction of that promotion.

Q: How frequently should I re-do my vision board?

A: Any time it feels right. I typically leave empty space on my vision board so I can adopt fresh items as they show up in my life, and add and reorganize throughout the year when I feel it. Trust me, you'll know. Then, each January, I give the board a complete refresh to get crystal clear about what I want in the new year. A few things remain, and a few have served their purpose and no longer cut the mustard.

What you'll need:

Any kind of board, if you're new to this perhaps begin with a cork board or poster board from the hardware store, they run about a dollar. If you can, I suggest a pin board or something pretty you like to look at.

Scissors, tape, pins, and a glue-stick to put your board together. If you want, fun pens, labels, or just about anything else you can think of to dress up your board. I do not use that stuff, however, if decorations make you feel good, then go all out.

Periodicals that you can snip photos and quotes from.

Most fundamentally, the things you want to look at daily. Photographs, quotes, phrases, pictures of locations you wish to go, reminders of occasions, places, or individuals, postcards from buddies and practically anything that will motivate you.

Time. Give yourself a hassle-free hour or more to put your board together.

Set the mood. Switch off the TELEVISION and put on some peaceful tunes. Light a candle and clear your space.

I will close this chapter with a little story about the focus of most people in life:

An American businessman was standing at the pier of a small coastal Mexican village when a small boat with just one fisherman docked. Inside the small boat were several large yellow fin tuna. The American complimented the Mexican on the quality of his fish.

"How long did it take you to catch them?" the American asked.

"Only a little while" the Mexican replied.

"Why don't you stay out longer and catch more fish?" the American then asked.

"I have enough to support my family's immediate needs" the Mexican said.

"But" the American then asked, "What do you do with the rest of your time?"

The Mexican fisherman said: "I sleep late, fish a little, play with my children, take a siesta with my wife, Maria, stroll into the village each evening where I sip wine and play guitar with my amigos. I have a full and busy life, senor."

The American scoffed: "I am a Harvard MBA and could help you. You should spend more time fishing and with the proceeds you could buy a bigger boat and, with the proceeds from the bigger boat, you could buy several boats. Eventually you would have a fleet of fishing boats. Instead of selling your catch to a middle-man, you would sell directly to the consumers, eventually opening your own can factory. You would control the product, processing and distribution. You would need to leave this small coastal fishing village and move to Mexico City, then LA and eventually NYC where you will run your expanding enterprise."

The Mexican fisherman asked: "But senor, how long will this all take?"

To which the American replied: "15-20 years."
"But what then, senor?"

The American laughed and said: "That's the best part. When the time is right, you would announce an IPO - an Initial Public Offering - and sell your company stock to the public and become very rich. You would make millions."
"Millions, senor? Then what?"

The American said slowly: "Then you would retire. Move to a small coastal fishing village where you would sleep late, fish a little, play with your kids, take a siesta with your wife, stroll to the village in the evenings where you could sip wine and play your guitar with your amigos..."

DOES LIFE WITHOUT ALCOHOL SUCK?

This question came from a couple of my Stop Drinking program members who were chatting on Facebook. They were agreeing with each other that a life without alcohol appears to be dull.

I can completely understand this thinking. I probably spent five years of my drinking life avoiding dealing with my addiction due to the same sort of thinking.

Alcohol was so deeply ingrained into my life that I simply couldn't see how I could function without it. I worried that I would have no way to relax, no way to socialize and even no way to get to sleep of a night.

The only thing I can tell you, having been on both sides of the coin is this. The worry that life is less without alcohol is just another illusion of the drug.

You have to marvel at the power of this poison. It has the potential to make you look at black and call it white. Alcohol brings nothing but misery and suffering and yet somehow it manages to persuade you that you can't live without it.

I wish I had the words to describe the difference between my happy sober life now and the fat, zombified existence that I insisted I 'enjoyed' as a drunk.

It's a frustrating problem for me personally, because I speak for a living. I spent over twenty years as a professional broadcaster and yet I can't describe just how much better my life is without alcohol. Perhaps the words don't exist!

I have mentioned repeatedly about the apparent downsides of alcohol addiction. The fact that it steals your money, time, health and relationships.

What I have never talked about before is the damage alcohol does to your spiritual health.

Wait… before you run away because I have gone all-spiritual on you. What I mean by spiritual is an inner state of peace and happiness. We as a species get a little confused between happiness and fun. I believe happiness comes from within and fun is just an external input.

Whether you are religious, spiritual or just open to meditation, the fundamental goal remains the same: To reduce the ego and spend more time in grateful appreciation of the present moment. True peace and happiness only exists in the 'now', never in the future or past.

Alcohol prevents you from achieving this aim. The alcohol addict is rarely in the moment. While they are consuming alcohol, they are sedated and prevented from being fully aware by the drug. When they are not drinking, they are plotting and planning when they will next be able to do so.

I recorded a video to go along with this chapter. I went to the beach where I got married fifteen years ago. The stunningly beautiful location I have been with my children and family many times in the past.

Until I went back to make the video, I can honestly say I have never really been there before. Let me explain that statement; sure I have been there physically, many times before. However, I was never really present mentally to appreciate the beauty around me.

All I was thinking was 'yes very good, when can we go back to the hotel.' It's not that the hotel was so fantastic that I couldn't bear to be parted from it. I think you know why I was so desperate to get back to the hotel.

Finally, when I stood on that beach sober and allowed myself to really experience the beauty of the place, a wave of peace washed over me. It almost brought a tear to my eye – a powerful moment I allowed alcohol to steal from me a million times over.

If you want to be sad live in the past if you want to be worried live in the future. Happiness and true peace exists only in the present moment.

Alcohol will do everything it can to prevent you from staying here.

What you will find is that after six months of sober living, you will look back on the question of whether 'life without alcohol sucks' and laugh until you are sick.

There is nothing I can say to persuade a drinker of this; all I can do is challenge you to experience it. I know you will come back to me full of shock, excitement and pure joy having experienced first hand what a sober life feels like.

HOW DO YOU STOP THINKING ABOUT DRINKING ALCOHOL?

When you get addicted to alcohol a lot of things change, and a lot of strange behaviors become reasonable to you. Drinkers think about drinking all the time.

If they are not drinking the stuff, they are planning when they can next. Addicts are constantly risk assessing every situation in life to make sure alcohol will be available should they want to drink.

This scary level of obsessive behavior becomes commonplace. But you only have to change the substance for the insanity to become apparent. Imagine if over a hundred times a day you thought about potatoes.

When you weren't eating them, you were planning where you can get your next fix of potato. If your friend invited you to a party and you found out that there would be no potatoes available. This would lead to a major tantrum and your refusal to attend.

If you were behaving like that around the humble spud on a daily basis. It wouldn't be long before your friends suggested medical intervention.

The human body is a fantastic thing. It will physically adapt and change to perform better tasks that you do regularly.

For example, in you decided to switch your writing hand, your body would eventually adapt to this change. After a decade of writing only with your left hand instead of the right you would find it strange and difficult to go back.

The same is true of habits and addictions. For decades you have been thinking about alcohol on a daily basis. Your mind expects this routine to be a part of your reality. So, don't be surprised if it doesn't stop as dramatically as you would perhaps prefer.

When you first quit drinking you will find alcohol or the lack of it is still on your mind often. This slowly fades away, but it will never go away completely.

A couple of days ago I stayed in a hotel I have not been to for over a decade. The last time I was there I remember checking in and getting the room key. But instead of going straight to the room I went out of the hotel to a convenience store. I bought a bag of chips and a massive bottle of Ouzo, which I planned to drink in the room.

This time I did head straight to the room after check-in. However, as soon as my foot crossed the threshold into the hotel suite, I had a powerful sensation come over me. I suddenly thought 'should I go an buy some Ouzo'?

Of course, as soon as I had the thought, I dismissed it as a terrible idea. However, you should be aware that even when you have been sober as long as me – these crazy thoughts still appear.

Some people get a little depressed about these sorts of thoughts. They worry that these mind farts are a sign that they have not really beaten the drug.

As with everything else in life you can't change the things you are not in control of. You can only change the way you respond to them.

For example, getting upset at the law of gravity won't make any difference to how it affects your body.

Instead of getting upset or angry when these thoughts occur, see them as a positive. They are little reminders that alcohol wants to pull you back into the trap.

Alcohol is like a little demon; you have not beaten him; you have locked him in a little box. He can't hurt you as long as you keep the box locked.

Occasionally he will shout out and beg you to put the key in the lock and give him a little air. Just like feeding a Gremlin after midnight, answering his plea is going to end in nothing but pain and misery for you.

Don't punish yourself for having these thoughts and don't feel bad about them. If you try and push them away or demand that they don't ever appear you actually make them stronger and more regular. Instead, when they appear, just acknowledge them, watch them unfold before you and then let them go.

WHAT ABOUT WHEN LIFE GETS BAD, VERY BAD?

Alcohol is treated as the go to panacea for all of life's major curve balls. Lose your job, get dumped by a partner or even suffer the agony of bereavement. You can be assured that a well-meaning friend or relative will reach straight for a stiff drink.

When people consider giving up booze for good there are many social aspects of the drug that they worry they will miss out on. But also it is common to be concerned that a coping mechanism will also be lost out on.

On the 4th July 2017 my ex-wife and mother of my two wonderful children died suddenly and unexpectedly. She was not ill, not a risk taker and only fifty years of age. Our world crashed down around us and for me personally the most difficult part of the whole horrible ordeal was watching my children suffer and not be able to do anything to pull them out of their torture.

You may wonder if at any point in this painful experience if I was tempted to drink. The honest answer is yes.

The days between Denise's death and the funeral felt intolerably long. Every minute felt like a week. As we waited for family and friends to fly in from around the world I woke every morning and tried desperately to fill the days with distractions for my children.

On the third day they were both visiting friends and I was left on my own in a hotel room for a good eight hours. I didn't want to be on my own and I didn't want my stupid brain to keep replaying events over and over again.

I briefly considered walking to a liquor store and buying a bottle of whiskey. The thought lasted no more than a few seconds before I quickly recognized that life was already hard enough without adding another problem.

Alcohol would have just made a bad situation worse. Plus, what I have learnt well in the past is; once you invite the monkey onto your back, he won't let go for a very long time. You will have to wrestle with him and prize his gnarled, devilishly strong fingers from your flesh one by one.

I believe that the vast majority of the drinkers I meet are intelligent individuals who are simply using alcohol to escape the harsh edges of life.

Get an unexpected bill – drink it away.
Mess things up at work – drink it away.
Miss out on the promotion – drink it away.
Argue with your partner – drink it away.

However, as I explain in Alcohol Lied to Me; booze doesn't fast forward you through stressful or painful events. It may appear that is what it is doing but in reality it just hits the pause button on life. When the drug wears off you are presented with the original problem but now you have an additional issue to deal with. That being, the withdrawal from a highly addictive drug.

In the case of my own personal experience recently. Grief has a natural process and as painful as it is you can't choose to skip any part of it.

My son is nineteen now but still very much a baby at heart. He absolutely adored his mother and he took her death very hard indeed. I had with me some prescription sedatives, but no matter how much he struggled with what was happening I resisted the urge to give him a tablet.

Experiencing the agony of the first four stages of grief are the only true route to the fifth and final phase, which is that of acceptance. Sedation would only delay that journey further.

The same is true of alcohol. You can drink and zombify yourself for a while but you can't cheat the system. The piper will have to be paid sooner or later. Nobody in their right mind would choose to pay later and extend the misery a second longer than is needed.

Once you get to the point where you accept that sobriety is a part of whom you are. Then you will start to feel immensely grateful in the dark times that you don't also have alcohol addiction to deal with.

You don't get a choice on this. Life is going to knock you down repeatedly; it is the nature of existence. Getting back up again is the only true choice. Getting back up sober is so much quicker and easier than trying to do so with a booze monkey clinging around your neck.

BE CONFIDENTLY YOU

You may be surprised to hear me say that I am not here to teach you how to be confident. Such a statement would imply that I know how to be confident and you don't. That is quite simply not true, and here is why: Everything you ever want to achieve is already inside you, your subconscious has the limitless power to manifest the life of your dreams. But you have to tell it what you want and without the ability to talk to it directly. I am sure you will agree that It doesn't matter how many times you order yourself to become wealthy it probably would not make a blind bit of difference. Think of your subconscious as a multi-billion dollar computer, that comes free when you are born but without an instruction manual. Xbox consoles only play games made for that specific console, it doesn't matter how hard you try to get it to play a game for the Nintendo WII it won't play ball. Your own internal super computer only runs programs placed into your subconscious in a very specific way. Now, these days I work with Apple Mac products because I they do everything I need them to and in a beautiful, reliable way. Some mornings I will go into my office and a little message will be flashing in the top right of my screen and it will say 'Mac OS updates have been successfully installed'. This is great news, my computer is not only bang up to date with the latest software but I had to do precisely zip to get it into this position. To be honest I never notice anything different after those updates have run and if it wasn't for the pop up alert I probably would never know anything had changed.

Let me tell you, the same thing is happening all the time to your own internal computer. Programs and updates are being installed all over the place; the only difference is you don't get the pop up message to advise you. Do something for me; think about an area of your life where you consider yourself to be lacking confidence. That belief structure was not with you when you were born it is a program that has been installed along the way. You probably don't remember when it was installed but if it exists in your life today then there absolutely must be a program in your subconscious generating it. The people who share our life and particularly our parents and teachers have implanted many of the programs in our head. Some of them are there by design and having the 'stranger danger' program installed may even have saved your life at some point. But not all programs serve us in a positive way. Researchers have discovered the average eighteen year old has been told 'no' or 'you can't do it' 147,000 times. Is it any wonder that you currently have some twisted thinking about confidence and self-esteem?

You are a confident person when you run the correct program. At the moment you are running a routine in your unconscious mind that says that you believe your self to be lacking in confidence – but this perception is just an illusion. You would probably agree with me that Wayne Rooney is a very confident and successful soccer player, Colin Keapernick is a very talented football player and Victor Marteniz is a superb baseball star of the MLB. But what do we mean by confident and why are they considered to be so much more worthy of the label than we give ourselves?

Let's take Wayne Rooney for example, last season he made one thousand eight hundred and ninety nine shots at goal in the UK

Premiership division. Of those eight hundred and ninety eight shots got nowhere near the goal! The total number of balls that came off his soccer boot and went into the back of the net was two hundred and eighty four! This means that eighty five percent of the shots Wayne Rooney makes miss the target – and yet we are certain in our belief that he is a confident soccer player. I don't know what you do for a living but I am willing to bet your success rate is much greater than fifteen percent.

What I want you to do is stop believing that you lack confidence or that failure isn't an option. Wayne Rooney never stops shooting at the goal. Every opportunity to score he gets, he takes. Without the hundreds and hundreds of misses he would not be able to achieve the hits and 'earn' his eighteen million dollars a year. Just in case you were wondering what that works out at per goal, it's sixty four thousand dollars for each one – no wonder he never stops shooting!

When you get out there and do the thing that scares you, whether that is making a presentation at work or approaching the hot girl in the supermarket – sometimes you are going to get a different outcome than you wanted. But be okay with that; understand that without those moments you can't be the person you want to be. It's okay to be okay and failure is a victory in its own right!

Once you can start living this new mindset what you will find is that the old programs in your head that were not serving you in a positive way get deleted and replaced. On my confidence bootcamps for guys, I sometimes challenge to go on a rejection mission. This is where you go out with the sole purpose of failing; I actually don't want you to succeed at this task. You might go up to the super hot, catwalk model and get blown out, that's great! I might ask you to interrupt a group of people chatting over lunch and tell them a joke that fails to make them laugh –

perfect, I love it! Get comfortable with failing, it's no big deal and what you will discover is nobody really cares. Once you get detached from the outcome then you are going to become more confident than you ever thought possible.

One more story to emphasize this important lesson and then I am going to give you two tricks to accelerate the process. A few months ago I was asked to consult for a telecoms company. They had a team of in house sales execs who each evening had to make random calls and cold sell the product to the person on the end of the line. I am sure you can imagine what a tough job this is and just how much abuse these guys take each day at work. As any salesman will tell you cold calling really sucks and no ambitious seller wants to do it a moment longer than they need to. For this reason this telecoms company had a very high turn over as staff. Literally as soon as the newbie salesman or saleswoman had cut their teeth on the cold calling they were applying for better sales jobs. On top of that a lot of the new recruits simply quit because they just couldn't handle the rejection of being told 'no' or worse hundreds of times a day. They asked me to advise on how these guys could be better motivated to deal with the negative responses they got from strangers on the end of the phone.

We worked out that it took on average seventeen rejections to get a sale. Obviously it didn't always work out like that and some salesmen performed better than others but roughly speaking they were selling a product every eighteen calls. So, we simply changed the way the new salesmen would be paid. Instead of getting a bonus when they sold a product we started paying them a small commission for every rejection they got and a bigger bonus for making the sale. What happened was amazing, the new salesmen actually started smiling when they got a 'no' or a slammed phone – because that previously negative event meant they just earned another dollar. My challenge to you right here and now is how do you think you can turn a current negative into a positive?

Of course it is a little easier to see the problem in other people than it is to see what is going wrong in yourself, but that doesn't mean you can't fix your own problems. If your problem is pushing yourself forward for promotion for example then I want you to be aware of what happens to make you procrastinate and ultimately fail to take the action required to get the promotion. Ask yourself, 'how do I know its time to procrastinate'? Obviously I don't know exactly what goes on in your head but lets use Graham as an example. Graham Roberts came to see me several years ago, he is a very talented architect but he was desperately unhappy at work. He was nudging fifty years old and still in a relatively junior position in his company. He felt he was punching well under his weight and was thoroughly depressed at the amount of money he was earning. I of course asked him why he kept getting overlooked for promotion and he said he thought it was because he never applied for any better jobs. Yeah that will do it, I said!

He explained that when he was fresh into the company, straight out of university he had been a bit cheeky and applied for a senior position even though he had only just landed the opening gig. He went through the interview process with the intention of demonstrating how ambitious he was. Unfortunately the department manager had taken it as an act of insolence and disrespect from the cocky new recruit. The interview went terrible and the manager ripped shreds off Graham, but worse than that for months afterwards he made sure Graham only got the work that nobody wanted to do. His fellow new starters were occasionally given bigger projects to work on and given the opportunity to shine while Graham kept being given the menial work that even a high school student wouldn't find a challenge. A few years later that manager left the company but Graham still kept his head down and did his best to avoid the attention of the department head. He said that over the years senior positions came up and he thought about applying but always chickened out at the last minute.

The first thing I asked Graham was 'how do you know it's time to chicken out'? He said, normally it is just after he fills out the paperwork and then knows that he has to take it down the corridor to the HR office. He said he has got right up to the door in the past before ripping it up and sometimes it is in the garbage before he even had chance to stand up from his desk. What Graham had created was a pattern, a series of events in his subconscious mind that are linked together like a line of dominos waiting to be pushed over. Filling out that application is anchored to a painful event and the ego responds to the triggering of that memory by trying to move him away from the source of the pain.

To break a pattern you have to first recognize that you have one and then consciously do something dramatically different to what the pattern wants to do. In Graham's case I asked him what he could do different and he came up with five or six alternatives including asking the intern to take the application form straight down the corridor, having his friend stand over him and take the application off him. He even suggested he could give his friend a hundred dollar bill and say 'if you don't see me take this application into the human resources office today – you have my permission to keep the $100'. I don't know which pattern interrupt he eventually used, but I do know that today he is several pay grades higher than he has ever been at before.

Think about your own life and see if you can spot any recurring events that you believe are holding you back or preventing you enjoying life to the full. As soon as the pattern starts to play out do something unexpected to break the state. This can be anything at all but it is better to make it something dramatically different. If you always start to feel panicky as soon as it is time to get on an aeroplane then instead of doing what you would normally do, sing happy birthday to yourself or wave your arms in the arm, make a sound like a chicken – do anything that breaks the pattern. Okay so you look crazy and you might not be able to do it for more than a few seconds because you are laughing so much, I don't care – you are breaking the pattern. It's like getting a steak knife and dragging it across a CD – eventually that CD will not play any more and eventually your pattern won't play like it did before.

You can also use this technique with other people who are operating in a state that isn't positive. Sometimes I meet people and no sooner have we shook hands do they start with a pity party about how terrible their life is and how low their confidence is. They are used to their friends and family responding with kind words and effectively joining the pity party. I never do this but I may jump up and down a bit or ask them if they can smell popcorn... I loved the confused expression on their face that says 'my old state is broken'. I don't want them to keep rerunning the broken patterns and so I don't let them – every time I get a sense that they are playing that old erroneous program I do something that they don't expect or just down right confuses them.

Parents... you can even use this technique on your children. I am sure you have experienced one of those embarrassing moments when your child has a tantrum (often they do it in a public place to make matters worse). They start kicking and screaming because they want something or don't want to go school. Ask yourself what happens next in the pattern, do you get angry and start shouting or do you have to hang your head and leave the place where it is happening? Whatever it is, do something different! Ask them how superman can fly, sing happy birthday, join in the protest or pull funny faces. Most times they will look at you with a beautifully confused expression, they are thinking 'what the hell are you doing mommy' but that's great because what they are not doing anymore is running the tantrum pattern.

The more tools you have in the box the more options will ultimately be open to you. Most people who come to see me know what they want but are trapped in a routine that they can't seem to break. They have these patterns and programs running that reduce their options down to only one or two possible outcomes. Ask yourself what else could you do and then set about installing the state you would need to get there. Another great tool for doing this is using meditation or hypnosis (which is really just a guided meditation). Hypnosis downloads are great for addressing very specific problems because we can use the subliminal commands like a laser guided missile to directly attack the incorrect beliefs hidden in your subconscious mind.

However, before you download and listen to any of these powerful tracks it is important that we ensure that you fully understand what hypnosis is, or more importantly what it is not. Hypnosis is not black magic, a party trick nor a piece of theatre. It is a naturally occurring process of the brain that has unfortunately attracted some seriously bad press over recent years; some might say even OJ Simpson has had better press than hypnosis! Thankfully, for over two thousand years it was documented and practiced with a great deal of respect. How bizarre that this long studied and amazing action of the human mind was essentially defamed by a man in a bar trying to convince girls to remove their clothes.

The traditional stage hypnotist is considered by most right thinking hypnotherapists and psychologists as a blundering incompetent dabbling in something they don't truly understand. If they did understand the amazing process they are playing with, I would suggest they would find something more productive to do with it than make a person believe they are a little fluffy duck called Roger!

A common misconception about hypnosis is that it is sleep. Although a hypnotized person appears to be sleeping, they are actually quite alert. Hypnosis is very difficult to describe, as nobody actually knows what is going on inside the mind of a subject. What we do know is that while in the trance state, the subject becomes very suggestible. A subject's attention, while they are going into trance, is narrowed down gradually.

Many areas of normal communication are removed one by one. Starting with sight, a person is asked to close his eyes and concentrate. Other senses are then removed from the equation; some people even lose complete feeling of their body. That may sound frightening, but it is accomplished in a slow, pleasant way, rather than suddenly turning off of a switch.

You enter a world of hyper relaxation and at the same time hyper awareness. As you might expect, as you remove certain senses the remaining ones become more acute to compensate. Often people who have been under hypnosis will come around and claim "it did not work". When you enquire as to why they believe hypnosis did not occur, they make statements such as "I could hear everything", "I could even hear the cars going past the window!" This is all part of the misconception that hypnosis is sleep, and that during trance you are unconscious, when in actual fact you are hyper conscious.

I am telling you about hypnosis not because I want you to take to the stage, but because I want you to understand the truly amazing power of the subconscious mind. A person in hypnosis is highly suggestible. The hypnotist has direct access to the person's subconscious without having to go through the conscious mind. This is how they can convince a six foot tall, 250lb man he is a light gentle ballet dancer and have him pirouetting his way around the stage.

Hypnosis is so natural, that you do it dozens of times a day without even realizing it. Have you ever driven home at the end of your working day and arrived home with no memory of the journey? Hypnosis just paid you a visit, your brain was using the opportunity of this familiar and fairly simple task to filter and file information in your brain.

You may notice yourself at work blankly staring at the computer screen in a deep peaceful daydream. This happens due to the vast amount of information constantly entering your brain, every few hours your mind must pause a little to filter and file all the information you have learned. Placing it in the correct storage area of the brain.

Many people find it helpful to pick one specific area to work on at a time. For example if public speaking is your biggest problem then download a hypnosis track that deals with this area and listen everyday exclusively to this track and do it for at least twenty one days before you move onto a new area of your personal development. During these powerful tracks I talk directly to your subconscious mind. I do this because I know that the conscious mind is a guard dog. The sort of animal the mail man must first distract before he opens the gate and creeps up the path to post the mail through the letterbox, after doing so he sneaks back out, hopefully without being noticed. During this book I have been directly talking to your guard dog, you can choose to accept what I am saying, or dismiss it. During hypnosis you do not have that problem; all suggestions are accepted without judgment because the words are directed to the subconscious.

A word of warning... Don't lie there waiting for something magical to happen, don't expect or demand anything, you will also need to be prepared to catch your ego trying to pull you out of the moment. It's fine when it does, if you find your mind wandering just notice what has happened, smile and refocus on the now. Relax and let the music and my words drift over you. There is nothing that you can do wrong, free yourself of that concern and let go of all expectation.

TIMELINE THERAPY

- Would you like to get rid of some emotional baggage?

- Are you troubled by hostile feelings?

- Would you like to get psychological control of your life?

- Have you ever been in a circumstance where somebody told you that you have overreacted to a situation, but you disagreed?

- Would you like to get clarity on what you desire in your life?

- Have you ever set objectives for the future and had them not happen?

- Would you like to find out how to picture your future, so it's more engaging, inspiring and exciting for you?

The result of our life experiences and the thoughts connected with them impact how we handle our daily lives. It's "the things" from our history that keeps us less than satisfied and stops us from accomplishing the outcomes we desire. You've got unlimited potential and Time Line Therapy ® provides you the resources to draw out your unseen abilities and desires and then guide you to the options you require to develop and make a brilliant, powerful future. Time Line Therapy ® uses the individual's own inner "Time Line" dealing with their Subconscious Mind in a variety of ways which includes healing psychological stress and getting rid of undesirable thoughts, feelings and habits in seconds instead of days, months or years. Time Line Therapy ® guarantees you can get free from the limiting beliefs of your past so that you start to live life like you mean it today.

Throughout history, humanity has been conscious of the movement of time. Aristotle was the first to point out the "flow of time" in his book Physics IV. William James mentioned linear memory storage as early as 1890. The most recent advancement in NLP is Time Line Therapy ® and it's methods are an exceptional and unrivaled technique for developing effective transformation in coaching, business, learning, and therapy.

Time Line Therapy ® is so strongly regarded that the Council of Psychotherapy in Croatia asked to be instructed in Time Line Therapy ® so they could help a lot of the victims of the war who were going through post-traumatic stress disorder.

Time Line Therapy ® has been so productive in generating good results that it has been used for over a decade by countless individuals including psychotherapists, mental health experts, life coaches, business coaches, and sports coaches. They use this technique to get rid of inappropriate psychological responses, like surges of temper, periods of lethargy, clinical depression, unhappiness, stress, and persistent worry, all of which are responsible for stopping individuals from accomplishing the lifestyle they wish for. You can use it to eliminate Limiting decisions or limiting beliefs, for instance, "I'm not good enough," "I'll never be wealthy," or "I do not deserve a wonderful loving relationship," every one of which generates incorrect limitations and hinder your capacity to create achievable results and objectives. Created by Dr. Tad James, Time Line Therapy ™ techniques allow you to get rid of numerous kinds of problems in your past, therefore allowing you to progress toward your objectives and aspirations.

At QUIT DRINKING BOOTCAMP I demonstrate how we use Time Line Therapy to go back and remove limiting beliefs that are holding us back in the present day. You can certainly use this process on yourself using the instructions below, but it is much better to have a trained Time Line therapist take you through the process.

At QUIT DRINKING BOOTCAMP I would ask you to sit comfortably, close your eyes and take in several deep, slow breaths.

Close your eyes and imagine that before you there is a line stretching out into the distance. This represents your life in the future. Imagine, if you turn around and look behind you, there is another line going way back to your birth. If you look backward you can see into the past, and if you look foward you can see the future.

Now imagine that you are floating gently backward, I want you to go to a happy moment within the last few weeks. When you are there, hover above the event and watch it unfold before you. You are floating above the scene dissociated from what is going on. This means you can see yourself in the image; you are watching it as though you are a third person.

Next, gently return to the present

Now, I want you to float into the future, just a couple of weeks to a happy event you can imagine happening. Float above the event and watch it unfold, enjoying all the positive emotions.

Now allow yourself to float higher and higher above your time line. So high that it feels like you are 30,000 feet in the air. When you look down on your timeline it's smaller now, just a few feet long.

Drop back down to your timeline and go backward to the first time you experienced the negative sensation you are here to fix. For example, if you want more self-confidence then go to the time in your past where you first had the confidence knocked out of you. Watch the whole event unfold, watch what happened and how everyone behaved.

Next, I want you to float a little further back to a point just before that event happened. Ask your subconscious mind what it learned from the event.

What else, what else, what else... keep asking until you have exhausted all the learning.

Ask yourself if the old emotions are still there. How do you now feel about that past event, has it changed?

Float forward now and return to the present moment and slowly open your eyes.

It is challenging to demonstrate how powerful this process is in a book, the audiobook will be better and the live event the ultimate experience. However, there are qualified Time Line Therapists all over the world, and if you would like to try this powerful healing process for yourself, I encourage you to get on Google and find your nearest master practitioner.

SECTION SEVEN
– LEARNING

THE FOUNDATIONS
OF SUCCESS

In the summer of 2009 my son and I nearly died. To this day I feel a considerable conflict of emotions about the day. I am proud that I was able to save my son's life and I am devastated that I failed to see the danger before it was too late. I was still living in England at the time, and we had taken an annual vacation in Cyprus where we had the villa. For a change of scene, we decided to travel to the west coast of the island and spend a few days in a nice hotel. We had stayed at this particular hotel before, back when my son Jordan was only three years old. He had found the concept of a hair drying chained to the wall fascinated and played with it all week, so on our return, we tried to recreate the image.

The hotel had a fantastic swimming pool but what made it special was its own private cove and glorious sandy beach. We remembered having great fun there, the waves would come rolling in increasing in speed and height, as the natural funnel shape of the cove squeezed the water tighter and tighter. So while my ex-wife and my daughter opted for the tranquility of the pool my son and I headed straight for the action of the beach. The perfect blue water was full of people, small children paddling and screaming with delight as the waves broke upon the golden sand. Teenagers and young adults knocked a ball back and forth a little further out; it was a perfect scene. I think the sheer number of people in the water made me either ignore or not see the red warning flags that had been raised to indicate that a dangerous riptide was occurring.

Jordan and I were having a blast diving over the waves and chasing each other in the wonderfully warm Cyprus sea. What we didn't realize is that we were very slowly pulled out to sea. We still had our feet on the sand at this point but every time we jumped up the current grabbed us and pulled us another foot deeper. As we were moving together at the same speed, neither one of us noticed that we were quickly becoming the furthest people out. Quite soon after this point, I realized that I was on my tiptoes and just about managing to stay in contact with the seabed. I understood that if I was nearly out of my depth, then Jordan was several feet from being able to stand. However, at this point I still wasn't at all worried, I just shouted to my son who was a few feet away that we should go back in a little.

We turned and started to swim for the shore, we swam for about three minutes, and when I stopped to put my feet down, expecting the sand to now be comfortably under my feet, I went completely under the water. Despite swimming hard for the shore we were now another six feet further out to sea, and I could no longer touch the bottom at all. A vast sensation of panic rushed through my body, and I screamed at Jordan to swim as hard as he could. We both dumped the breaststroke and through all our energy into kicking and crawling our way back. After another few minutes of frantic swimming, I stopped once more to check the depth of the water and to see how much progress we had made. To my devastation, we were again even further out to sea. I was tired and struggling to keep my head above water, I shouted for help, but I knew the noise of the rolling waves would mean you probably wouldn't hear us if you were ten feet away. There were no lifeguards on the beach, and nobody was sitting keeping an eye on us.

At that moment I honestly thought we were going to die. Even as I sit here writing about the incident, which was a decade ago now, I feel that horrible knot in my stomach that I experienced back then — the realization that my son was going to die and it was all my fault. I didn't care that I was going to die too, the only thoughts I had in those awful seconds of acceptance is that my son is going to drown and there is nothing I can do to stop it. As if I ever need more evidence that your subconscious will come up with some pretty surprising answers if you ask the right question, here it was. I certainly didn't consciously come up with this idea; I just started doing it. I dropped down under the water until my feet hit the sand, there was about three foot of sea above my head by this point, but I could grab hold of my sons legs and then dig my feet into the sand and push him forward until I ran out of breath. At which point I would scramble to the surface and take another lungful of air. I was using vast amounts of energy with each cycle, and despite the enormous effort, I was only moving Jordan about six inches closer to shore each time. But for the first time, I was heading in the right direction. Over and over again I dropped to the bottom and nudged him forward; it took around twenty minutes of this before I could touch the bottom and keep my head above water at the same time. It felt more like four hours, but the relief of being able to stand again was overwhelming. I grabbed my son and dragged him to the beach where we both collapsed.

We lay exhausted for a few minutes without speaking. Eventually, I turned my head to Jordan and said 'do you know what just happened'? He looked me in the eye and said 'Yes Dad, we nearly died.' I don't think I will ever forget how I felt at that moment — a tidal wave of relief, pride, and guilt all at once. I saved my son, but I couldn't help but beat myself up for failing to protect him from the danger in the first place.

I later found out that the locals refer to that beautiful sandy cover as 'Killer Beach' and at least two or three tourists die every year in the same spot. Swept out to sea by the deadly current that rages under the perfect cobalt waters. The point of this story is a lack of knowledge can sink you. I now know that the way to escape a riptide is not to swim against it but to traverse across it until you reach a point where it's not so strong. You may have to swim several hundred feet down the coast, but eventually, you will reach the end of the swell and be able to swim safely ashore. In short, my son and I could have very easily died that day purely down to a lack of knowledge. It was not that the challenge before us was impossible, but we did not have the skills to confront it.

So many people dream of a different life. They want to escape the rat race and run their own enterprise. They want to find their soulmate and have a genuinely beautiful relationship; they want to find their purpose in life and spend every day from now on doing what they love and getting paid for it. However, the vast majority of people want someone to make it easy for them. There is no shortcut to glory; I would love to win the lottery one day, but I know that the chances are pretty low considering I don't ever buy a ticket. What this says about me is winning the lottery is a 'nice to have' but not a 'must have.' By this point in the book, you should have some pretty clearly defined goals, what I encourage you to do now is think about what you don't know, that you don't know. If you want to be a success at something you must learn it to the point where you could teach it to someone else.

Part of the process I take my Stop Drinking Expert members through is learning how the drug is manipulating them. Previously most people have attempted to quit drinking on their own, but virtually always by using willpower alone. This is an approach to problem drinking that has a 95% chance of failure; it is exactly like getting caught in a riptide and opting to swim against the current. I show problem drinkers how the illusion is being performed, and it's a bit like going to see a magic show by Penn and Teller. The first time you see the illusion you are blown away, it looks and feels like you just witnessed real magic being performed. However, when they come back onto the stage and show you exactly how the trick was done, it ceases to be magic and transforms into a piece of theatre. It doesn't matter how long you live; you will never be able to see that same illusion performed again and see it with the same wonder you did the first time.

Often it's the information that you don't know you don't know that is key to your success. For example, I have had a YouTube channel for over a decade, I have occasionally made the odd video and thrown it up there. However, I have never seen a vast amount of success from my efforts and have never given it much thought or attention. I will admit to being a little miffed at seeing people creating similar content to me getting ten times the views and subscribers but I could never work out how they were so much more successful. Then about three months ago a famous YouTuber with half a million subscribers messaged me. She said 'I love your videos, they are amazing BUT what the hell are you doing with your YouTube strategy.' She said that I was making dozens of fundamental mistakes in every video I uploaded and offered to coach me on what I was doing wrong'. Since Natasha jumped in and repaired my massive gap in knowledge, my subscriber growth has accelerated tenfold.

This is the knowledge that is hugely valuable. So I encourage you to take your goals and objective and dismantle them into a thousand pieces. I want you to find out how every detail of your plan fits together, leave no nut, bolt or screw in place. You will be surprised at what you discover, and when you identify an area, you need to expand your knowledge on, pursue it relentlessly. If you are serious about living to your full potential, there should not be a moment where you are not growing, learning and developing. You probably won't be surprised to hear that another common trait shared by the vast majority of the world's most successful people is they watch a tiny amount of television. There is an excellent reason they call it 'the idiot box.'

Successful people read a lot of books, take a lot of courses and subscribe to something called Automobile University. If you have any sort of commute to work, this is the perfect opportunity to be learning and driving yourself forward. However, most people listen to music or the nonsense coming out of the radio. I was a commercial radio broadcaster for over a decade, and I can tell you that you can write on one page the value information I delivered over that period. Most of what I was told to talk about was celebrity gossip and speculation about who would win X-Factor this year - total garbage. Any spare opportunity you get should be spent excitedly learning. The results are outstanding, it is said that if you listen to a personal development audiobook every day on the way to work and then again on the way home. Within a few years, you will have learned as much as a standard university degree course.

THANK YOU

Coming to a city near you soon
www.StopDrinkingExpert.com/Quit-Drinking-Bootcamp/

Thank you for reading Unleashed From Alcohol with me. I sincerely hope the techniques, tools and systems in this book result in hugely powerful change in your life. I have never met you but I know for sure that if I did, within a few moments I would discover something amazing about you. I know this because I have never met anyone where that didn't happen. You are already in a unique situation. It is said that somewhere around 80% of the people who by a self-improvement book like this never even open it. The fact that you are here at the end speaks volumes about your passion and commitment to change.

Remember life is not something that happens to you, that is how the passengers think and explain away their failure to live with passion, peace and purpose. Life is something that happens for you, everything is conspiring to provide the most beautiful and amazing experience here on earth. Approach each day with the sneaking suspicion that life is out to do you good. Stop being so hard on yourself, and see the pure untapped potential bubbling away under the surface.

I wish you a truly exceptional life, full of happiness, peace and purpose.

Before we go our separate ways, can you help me spread this message a little further today? If you could do a couple of things (or all if you prefer) on this little list it would make a monumental difference and I would be eternally grateful.

1. **Go back to the digital store you bought this book and leave a rating and review.**
2. **Follow me on Facebook or Twitter and leave me a review there too. I always read them and comment back.**
3. **Go to website and join my free How To Quit Drinking webinar or even book your place on the next QUIT DRINKING BOOTCAMP event**
4. **Tell your friends about this book**

Anyone of those little acts would be fantastic. Once again thank you for trusting me and I hope today is the beginning of an awesome new life.

Craig Beck

Websites:
www.CraigBeck.com
www.StopDrinkingExpert.com

Social Media
https://www.facebook.com/craigbeckbooks/
https://twitter.com/craigbeck

OTHER BOOKS BY CRAIG BECK

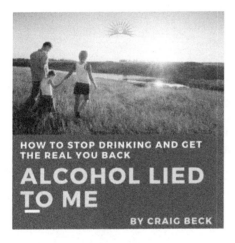

Alcohol Lied To Me

Craig Beck is a well-regarded family man with two children, a lovely home and a successful media career; a director of several companies, and at one time the trustee of a large children's charity, Craig was a successful and functioning professional man in spite of a 'two bottles of wine a night' drinking habit. For 20 years, he struggled with problem drinking, all the time refusing to label himself an alcoholic because he did not think he met the stereotypical image that the word portrayed.

He tried numerous ways to cut down; attempting 'dry months', banning himself from drinking spirits, only drinking at the weekend and on special occasions (and found that it is astonishing how even the smallest of occasions can suddenly become 'special').

All these 'will-power' based attempts to stop drinking failed (exactly as they were destined to do). Slowly he discovered the truth about alcohol addiction, and one by one, all the lies he had previously believed started to fall apart. For the first time, he noticed that he genuinely did not want to drink anymore. In this book, he will lead you though the same remarkable process.

The Craig Beck method is unique...
• No need to declare yourself an alcoholic.
• A permanent cure, not a lifetime struggle.
• No group meetings or expensive rehab.
• No humiliation, no pain and 100% no 'will-power' required.
• Treats the source of the problem, not the symptoms.

Alcohol Lied to Me has already helped thousands of people to escape from alcohol addiction. It has been translated into several different languages and has topped bestseller charts around the world. Newly updated, this third edition of the book includes two new chapters.

https://www.stopdrinkingexpert.com